A Bob Hamrdla,
avec mon amitié,
Caen, Oct. 10, 2011
André Heintz

IF I MUST DIE...

D0899704

Gérard FOURNIER - André HEINTZ

From "Postmaster" to "Aquatint"

The Audacious raids of a British commando 1941 - 1943

Collection
Des Souvenirs et des Hommes

OREP
EDITIONS

English translation : Heather Costil

FOREWORD

In June 1940, Great Britain was the only nation that bravely continued to face up to Nazi Germany and Fascist Italy.

All of the possible resources were utilised to gain information on the enemy's intentions, on its military organisation and its defence systems. Resistance movements and intelligence networks were gradually set up in Europe and they partly contributed to providing such information.

The enemy also needed to be shaken, to be made uneasy via secret, brutal and unexpected operations.

These missions were the work of Commando units comprising the bravest of volunteers who were trained and skilled for such perilous feats, many of which only came to light after the end of the war. One of them took place on the Calvados coast on the 13th of September 1942. Its code name was "Aquatint". The Commando in charge of the operation comprised eleven men from the "Small Scale Raiding Force".

The course of the operation was to be tragic. All of the mission's components: its preparation, the commando's composition, the enemy-controlled coastal approach, the confrontation, the enemy reaction and the outcome are recounted in this book written by two perfectly qualified authors.

André Heintz, a Volunteer Resistance Fighter was a successive member of several French Resistance Networks. He is the author of several works on the Resistance and the Liberation, and has extensive knowledge of specialised British archives.
Gérard Fournier is a historian and history teacher and has also written a number of works on the Resistance and deportation. With perseverance and talent, he has carried out painstaking research to reconstitute the story of this commando and of each of the men who took part in it.

André Heintz and Gérard Fournier have pulled together their resources and their expertise to write this book in the aim of bringing out of oblivion the courage, the sacrifice and the names of these men.

We thank them sincerely for the narration of this tragic raid. We also fully appreciate the audacity and the vigilance of our British allies who were relentlessly committed to obtaining information on the enemy whom they constantly tried to subvert.

Finally, let us emphasise the coincidence of history: on that same beach, renamed "Omaha Beach", two years later the 1st and the 29th Infantry Divisions of the American Army were to land during the greatest ever amphibious operation of military history on the 6th of June 1944.

Thanks to this work, the memory of operation "Aquatint" will live on and we will also remember with admiration and profound respect those men, led by Major Gustavus March-Phillips, who fell on the beach of Saint-Laurent-sur-Mer.

Vice-President of the Confédération Nationale
des Combattants
Volontaires de la Résistance*
President of the Calvados Section

Jacques VICO

* National Confederation of
Volunteer Resistance Fighters

Part one:

THE MEN FROM THE
62ND COMMANDO

CHAPTER I
FROM THE *MAID HONOR FORCE*
TO THE *SMALL SCALE RAIDING FORCE*

"I'm ashamed of this withdrawal. Aren't you?"

Stretched out on the sandy beach of Dunkirk, Captain Gustavus March-Phillips contemplated sombrely the man who had just fired this disquieting question at him. The officer immediately introduced himself,

"Captain Geoffrey Appleyard, Royal Army Service Corps. I'm from Yorkshire".

March-Phillips propped himself up on his elbows and observed his companion with increased attention; he was evidently far younger than himself. He was a man of fine features, chestnut coloured hair, brown eyes, a high forehead, a straight nose, a wide mouth with a distinct contour, and a small dimple on his chin. Clearly a very handsome man.

Two hours of conversation followed, at the end of which the two officers had sealed a genuine and

Geoffrey APPLEYARD

Geoffrey Appleyard, *in Major's uniform, undated. (Photo taken from* Anders Lassen, VC, MC, of the SAS *by Mike Langley, New English Library, London, 1988). This photograph is displayed on the fireplace of the* **Village Memorial Hall** *in Linton-on-Wharfe, Yorkshire.*

mutual friendship. Geoffrey was the eldest son of one of the most prominent families of Linton-on-Wharfe near Wetherby, whose residence was resided at Manor House. He had graduated from Cambridge with an engineering degree. Geoffrey's father, M.J.E. Appleyard was director of Appleyard Limited, Motor Engineers in Leeds, and counted heavily on his eldest son to take over the, then small, family business. However, just three days before war was declared, he could do nothing to prevent his son from signing up with the British Expeditionary Force and heading off for France. Consequently, Geoffrey's sister, Joyce, decided that she too would sign up with the "F.A.N.Y." (First Aid Nursing Yeomanry), a female British army corps, essentially involved in caring for transmission services.

Despite the fact that he was eight years his senior, March-Phillips quickly discovered that he had several things in common with Appleyard: his liking for adventure and risk and his passion for sport and energetic open-air activities. March-Phillips was tall, dark and of athletic build. With his eyelids drooping slightly over his brown almond-shaped eyes, dominated by a very high forehead and his hair combed back, he still had a certain charm despite the few imperfections caused by his intrepidity. Among such souvenirs were a slightly hooked nose caused by his many falls from his horse, and his somewhat protruding ears which he had trouble concealing, as well as a scar on his upper lip. Before the war, he had joined the British-Indian Army, but in 1931 he decided to leave. Gustavus was a naturally talented writer. In one of his novels entitled "Ace High", he described a young English soldier in the Colonial Forces of the 1920's; a soldier with a considerable resemblance to Gustavus himself: adventurous and restless, the young soldier abruptly cut short his military career and auctioned his personal belongings to pay his fare back to England. Gustavus March-Phillips is also known to have written three other novels in which he endeavoured to share his passion for hunting, horse-riding and navigating. Then came the war, and he signed up for the army again, in the Expeditionary Forces, just like Geoffrey Appleyard, within the Royal Artillery.

Geoffrey and Gustavus were repatriated to England together, thanks to operation Dynamo which made possible the rescue from the Nazi clutches of some 300,000 men, of whom 110,000 Frenchmen, and from that moment on, they never lost sight of each other. Both men wanted to fight against the Hitlerian enemy, but in their own manner, if possible avoiding rigid rules and regulations and officious army discipline.

In the autumn of 1940, March-Phillips heard about the creation of special commandos and eventually decided to apply. A letter to his friend Tim Alleyn conveyed his feverish impatience whilst he awaited a reply from his hierarchy,

"Dear Mate, I've been recommended for the post of a commando leader, but owing to a fatuous major in

A branch, I was unable to get the forms directly to Eastern Command. It has to go round the Corps tip and they take a week. So HO won't get it until too late unless you can tell them what has happened. The thing arrived here late in the first place, and they sat on it in the office. My God, they are awful. Anyway, I've been recommended a second time, and could you tell them that? If I come up for an interview, we'll have a terrific dinner. I'm feeling much too well, terribly fit, and nothing to do..." [1]

He finally obtained satisfaction. As soon as he was recruited as Commando Troop Leader of the 7th Commando, one of Lord Louis Mountbatten's Combined Operations units, his first thoughts went out to his friend Geoffrey. He needed a second officer. Captain Appleyard, who had recently received the Military Cross for heroism during combat preceding the withdrawal from Dunkirk, appeared to March-Phillips to be the most appropriate candidate to put forward to his superiors. In one of his letters to Geoffrey, Gustavus wrote,

"It's absolutely terrific. It's the grandest job in the army that one could possibly get. Just think of operating under direct orders from the C-in-C. No red tabs, no paper work, none of all the things that are so cramping and infuriating and disheartening in the army". [2]

---

[1] *Letter transcribed for a radio recording for the BBC on the 20th of August 1971, **"If any question why we died** (A quest for March-Phillips)". Further reading in Part Four, Chapter II.*
[2] *Idem.*

Geoffrey needed no further convincing and he immediately accepted his friend Gus's offer.

Over the following weeks and months, March-Phillips took to recruiting a small group of men: Lieutenants Graham Hayes, Colin Ogden-Smith and John Pinkney, Sergeants Leslie Wright, Leslie Prout and two Danes, Anders Lassen and Jan Nasmyth. All of these men needed to receive specific training in commando techniques: marches, combat and navigation. The officer was given carte blanche and very much appreciated this independence.

The group set off for a small period to train on the western coast of Scotland, however the appalling weather with torrential rain almost every day rendered the men totally inactive and they eventually moved to Dorset. In Poole, March-Phillips, preferring not to totally depend on the Royal Navy, set out in search of a boat on which he could train his troops. In Brixham Harbour, he requisitioned an old 35 ton trawler called Maid Honor. The trawler had been built by Jackmans Yard shipbuilders in Brixham in 1925-1926 on behalf of Charles Stanley Howe. In 1936, it was sold for £600 to Commander W. Bertram Bell, a member of the Royal Yacht Squadron, who had spent some £3,000 to have the trawler converted into a yacht[3]. He gave more

---

[3] In 1926, the **Maid Honor** won the Wallace Challenge Cup **(Mule class)**, during the Brixham-Torbay regatta. Despite stormy weather, Charles Howe's crew sailed the yacht three times round the race circuit, covering some 30 miles in less than three hours, which was quite an achievement.

Gustavus March-Phillips in civilian clothes, photograph taken before the war, no place, no date. Smaller picture: Gustavus March-Phillips in his Lieutenant's uniform, undated. (Photo taken from Anders Lassen, VC, MC, of the SAS by Mike Langley, New English Library, London, 1988).

height to the cabins by recovering space from the ballast, had an auxiliary motor fitted and replaced the tiller with a steering wheel. Twenty metres long, 4.4 metres wide, with a 2.3 metre water draught, the boat immediately appealed to March-Phillips, who sent Anders Lassen and five other men from the Commando to collect it and bring it back to Wareham.

In the spring of 1941, the small troop commenced training on the Maid Honor which March-Phillips sailed up and down the Dorset coast day and night come rain or shine. After each outing, the trawler was moored at Russel Quay on the Arne Peninsula, an inconspicuous location far from Poole's main harbour. The Maid Honor's solid framework conferred the vessel with excellent sea performance.

The months went by and March-Phillips was finally ready to cast off. However, he had received no authorisation from the Admiralty, neither to sail any farther than the coastal waters, nor to implement the highly targeted and localised attacks he planned on enemy territory. Hence, he waited for permission to execute the plan that had been prepared with the Dutch section of the S.O.E, the Special Operations Executive. This very secret service was rival to the Intelligence Service and had been entirely set up in August 1940 following a decision by the Prime Minister Winston Churchill himself. The SOE's director of operations and training, and later executive director, was Major General Sir Colin Gubbins, one of the rare subversion experts who,

Maid Honor

The Maid Honor Photograph taken from the bowsprit mast by Graham Hayes. In the fore-ground, Geoffrey Appleyard in a bathing suit, and "Marco", a Yugoslavian, spring 1940. (Photo taken from Anders Lassen, VC, MC, of the SAS by Mike Langley, New English Library, London, 1988).

The Maid Honor ▶ Photograph taken during a pre-war regatta, undated. (Photo taken from The Commandos 1940-1946 by Charles Messenger, William Kimber, London, 1985).

before the war, had written "The Art of Guerrilla Warfare" and "Partisan Leaders Handbook" as well as a pamphlet, translated into several languages, on how to use super-explosives. His military skills included extensive field experience. During the Norway Campaign, he had commanded small independent units, more or less forerunners to the Commandos, who, from fishing boats, carried out raids behind the enemy lines.

March-Phillip's plan immediately appealed to the SOE's military chief and he recruited the Commander of the 7th Commando in March 1941. The plan, according to its author, was to sail a fishing boat into a major harbour, to berth a German warship in port and to sink it with a grenade-launcher hidden on board. However, in 1941, the plan was considered to be too dangerous and insufficiently convincing, and the Admiralty refused it being put into action.

General Gubbins then decided to transfer the Maid Honor and its crew to West Africa and to entrust them with a specific mission: the inspection of the creeks and coves of French territories under the control of the Vichy Army. The British Admiralty suspected German U-Boats of fuelling up there and collecting food supplies between two attacks of allied convoys crossing the Atlantic.

Before leaving, March-Phillips received permission to make major modifications to the Maid Honor endowing the vessel with discreet and appropriate arms, thus rendering her apt to accomplish her mission. A retractable deck house, dissimulating two Vickers MK 8 heavy machine guns, was therefore installed. At the bow, a 4-tube anti-submarine grenade-launcher was installed under a pile of fishing nets. At the stern, a two-pounder gun was hidden between the wheel and the cabin. The deck and the gunwale were armour-plated. And finally, in the masting, each crow's nest was equipped with machine guns.

Thus adorned, the Maid Honor cast off from Poole harbour on the 10th of August 1941 with a crew of seven men. General Gubbins, together with a veritable areopagus of superior officers who had also made the trip from London, personally made his way to Poole to watch the departure of the Maid Honor Force, for that was to be the Commando's new name, specially given by the SOE for its first official mission. March-Phillips turned the engine on, then had all of the old trawler's sails hoisted, to add a certain panache to their departure and to take to the sea as quickly as possible. His apparent calm contrasted with the nervousness and even the apprehension of the other crew members. Just before casting off, Anders Lassen whispered to his compatriot, Jan Nasmyth, *"We're heading straight for death..."* In addition to Captain March-Phillips, the crew comprised Lieutenant Graham Hayes, Dennis Tottenham, Buzz Perkins and three Danish soldiers including Anders Lassen who was the team's only professional sailor. In civilian attire, Captain Geoffrey Appleyard, Sergeant Tom Winter and the other members of the Maid Honor Force were the most inconspicuous travellers on a liner travelling from Holland to the United States, and calling at Freetown in Sierra Leone on the 20th of August.

The Maid Honor's journey was relatively incident free. March-Phillips was, however, obliged to call at Dartmouth to disembark two of the three Danes; the inefficient navigator and another poor sailor who was suffering from the most appalling sea-sickness. After having called, on the 14th day, at the port of Funchal on Madeira Island, the Maid Honor continued her journey under sail and finally arrived in Freetown on the 21st of September 1941 under the flag of Sweden.

As soon as Appleyard learned of her arrival, he literally exulted, *"When I arrived at Lagos, I got the best piece of news I've ever had in my life - that is that Graham, and M.P. and the others have arrived at Freetown after an excellent voyage. I was enormously thrilled and literally shouted with joy. I don't think it would be exaggerated to say that it's one of the finest efforts of its kind in recent years"*.

After a jovial reunion, the eleven members[4] of the Maid Honor Force took their quarters at Lumley Beach. March-Phillips gave them orders to keep them occupied until such times as he received the go ahead to start the operation against Fernando Po Island, of

---

[4] *Gustavus March-Phillips, Geoffrey Appleyard, Graham Hayes, Anders Lassen, André Desgrange, Tom Winter, Dennis Tottenham, Franck Perkins, Robin Duff, Leslie Prout, Jack Taylor.*

which only he and Appleyard were aware. Some of the crew members were sent to collect food supplies, rum and various other provisions; others were responsible for totally servicing the Maid Honor (caulking, painting, interior and exterior cleaning).

During the months following the Maid Honor's overhaul, the troop made regular expeditions up and down the coast of the Gulf of Guinea, officially in search of possible German supply bases. The reality was that the troop's commander and his second officer wished to train their men and to maintain the excellent unity of the group.

Meanwhile, Colonel Louis Franck, head of NEUCOLS (Neutral Colonies) was exerting great pressure on the British Government to obtain permission to attack all ships of the Axis Forces who sought shelter in the neutral harbours of West Africa. And yet, two ships had been harbouring for 14 months in the neutral Spanish port of Santa Isabel, on Fernando Po Island, in the heart of the Gulf of Guinea. One of them, the Duchessa d'Aosta, was a 7,872 ton[5] Italian liner built in May 1921 by the Trieste shipyards; the other, the Likomba, was a 200 ton German tugboat. By the end of August 1941, an initial plan emerged to capture the German tugboat and to immobilise the Italian ship by sabotaging its propellers. But the British

---

[5] **Ton:** *International unit of volume used to determine the capacity of ships; one ton = 2.83m³.*

23

Government in London was hesitant. Endless discussions took place between the Admiralty and the Foreign Office, for the planned operation, which was to take place in a neutral port, should in no way bear prejudice to the British Government. Permission was finally given by the Foreign Office on the 12th of November 1941. The Admiralty followed on the 20th of November after Louis Franck had travelled to London to obtain the decision from the highest British authorities. A little later, a message was sent to Admiral Willis, Commander-in-Chief of the South Atlantic Station in Sierra Leone, in order for him to offer the necessary technical support.

The SOE had a local agent, Leonard Guise, who was responsible for the delivery of diplomatic mail between Lagos and Fernando Po. It was Guise who informed March-Phillips that the *Duchessa d'Aosta's* Captain had returned to Italy and that the ship was under the responsibility of its second in command. He also received confirmation from the local British chaplain, who had managed to have himself invited to a reception on board, under a false Spanish identity, that the spirits of the crew were pretty low and that many of them were suffering from venereal disease. A small detail clearly illustrated the crew's state of mind: all of the ship's bronze trimmings had been dismantled and sold by the sailors themselves.

Boosted by such information, March-Phillips received orders to set out for Lagos with the Maid

Operation POSTMASTER

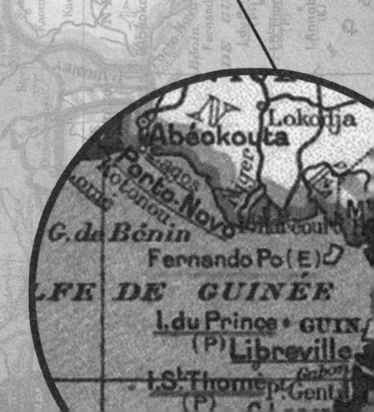

Map of the Island of Fernando Po (Spanish Guinea), from the Schrader &
Gallouédec Classical Atlas, Librairie Hachette, Paris, 1932.

Honor on the 14th of December. Colonel Franck's replacing officer, Commander Laversuch was in charge of elaborating and implementing the finer details of the operation. Swiftness and surprise were to be the main ingredients of its success. The following plan was therefore put forward: the commando was to enter into the harbour on a dark moonless night aboard a tug and a launch. The first boat was to take on the Duchessa d'Aosta and the second, the Likomba. Distinct groups were to, simultaneously, put out of action the Italian ship's radio, suppress any attempt at resistance, cut the mooring ropes using explosives and rapidly prepare the vessel for towing. The entire operation, from boarding the attacked vessels to their departure, was to take no longer than fifteen minutes. They were then to be transported to Cotonou, to await further escort by a Royal Navy ship towards an arranged meeting point. To reduce to a minimum possible resistance, it was hoped that the majority of the Italian crew of 44 men would be on land at the time of the attack. However, for security's sake, the Maid Honor's crew was increased to 32 men. Four men were recruited among the leading members of the Neucols organisation, and permission was requested for 17 additional men from the military personnel of General Giffard, Commander-in-Chief of West Africa. Captain March-Phillips was officially designated as the operation's commanding officer. Initially planned for the 22nd of December, the operation was postponed to the 14th of January at midnight.

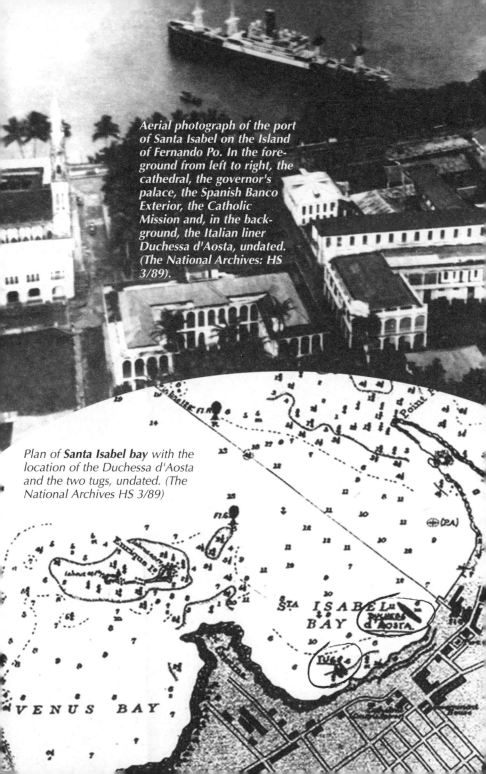

Aerial photograph of the port of Santa Isabel on the Island of Fernando Po. In the foreground from left to right, the cathedral, the governor's palace, the Spanish Banco Exterior, the Catholic Mission and, in the background, the Italian liner Duchessa d'Aosta, undated. (The National Archives: HS 3/89).

Plan of **Santa Isabel bay** with the location of the Duchessa d'Aosta and the two tugs, undated. (The National Archives HS 3/89)

Operation POSTMASTER

▲
*A few men from the **Maid Honor Force** at their **Nigerian encampment** during preparations for operation **Postmaster**.*
From left to right:
Peter Kemp, Leslie Prout, André Desgrange and Jack Taylor,
late 1941.
(Private collection)

The operation was given the code name: Postmaster. Commander Laversuch was responsible for informing the British Vice Consul in Fernando Po of the details of the operation and he obtained his approval at the beginning of December. The Nigerian Governor also approved the operation on the 20th of December and, on behalf of the Nigerian government, loaned the Vulcan tugboat and the Nuneaton launch together with their crews.

Whilst, in Lagos, detailed preparations for operation Postmaster were underway, the Royal Engineer Captain Richard Lippett, one of the SOE officers posted at Santa Isabel, was busy preparing the terrain. Officially, he worked for the Liverpool shipping firm run by John Holt in Fernando Po. Lippett used one of his agents, an anti-Falangist Spaniard, to organise two dinner parties for the officers and crew members of both of the Axis vessels. The first was aimed at allaying suspicion, but the second, planned on the 14th of January, was aimed at keeping as many crew members as possible on land.

On the dawn of the 11th of January, the Vulcan and the Nuneaton left Lagos with two groups on board. During the night of the 13th of January, March-Phillips' men continuously rehearsed their respective roles in the operation that was to take place in the middle of the night, in the port of Santa Isabel, and that was to enable them to capture the Italian ship and the German tugboat.

The following day, the Maid Honor Force arrived within sight of the Spanish port an hour earlier than planned. March-Phillips had forgotten the one-hour time difference between Spain and Lagos. At 23.00 hours local time, the port and the town were still lit up. The Vulcan and the Nuneaton would have to linger in the shadows until midnight struck. But March-Phillips' patience was pushed to the limit, and, without waiting for the lights to go out, he ordered the commanders of both boats to commence their approach into the port. The tugboat, the larger of the two vessels, set out towards the Duchessa d'Aosta, and the smaller boat headed for the Likomba.

On land, the dinner party in honour of some thirty Italian and German officers was in full swing and alcohol was flowing freely.

Already berthed alongside the Italian merchant ship, the Vulcan's crew headed by Anders Lassen, nimbly climbed up the small ladder leading to the promenade deck. They were all armed with a dagger, a truncheon and a pistol; however orders had been given to avoid at all costs the use of firearms. If necessary, two Bren light machine guns were aimed and ready to fire from the deck of the Vulcan. Suddenly, one of the men, Desmond Longe, let slip a curse as he stumbled on something soft on the deck. His surprise was to be overwhelmed by his incredulity; he had just run into a pig that the Italian sailors had left free on the ship's deck. Two other pigs were then found on the rear deck.

The men from the first group had found no-one on board, the night watchman having jumped into the sea from the crow's nest as soon as he saw them approaching. March-Phillips rushed inside with a few men, ran through the gangways, stopping at each deck and taking prisoner the 27 crew members and one woman left on board. Meanwhile, Appleyard, who had just made an eight foot leap on board, had already placed two explosive charges on the anchor chains with the help of the boatswain, Desgrange. The first exploded around 23.35 hours, but the second totally failed to accomplish its mission. Without checking whether the fuse was still burning or not, the British officer, aware that the success of the entire mission depended on his speedy intervention, needed no more than a minute to set another explosive charge. Lassen and his group immediately set about hoisting the heavy hawser on deck.

Meanwhile, armed with an automatic pistol, Captain Hayes and his men captured the Likomba tanker together with a 70 ton barge, the Bibundi, which happened to be berthed alongside the German tugboat. The watchman, as well as the few crew members, had immediately fled by jumping overboard. In the same manner as for the Duchessa d'Aosta, explosives were placed on the anchor chains of both vessels. Graham Hayes and Sergeant Tom Winter were in charge of operations. Shortly afterwards, the explosives freed them from their mooring ropes and the Nuneaton immediately started to slowly tow them out of the port.

The manoeuvre proved to be somewhat more delicate on the Vulcan. The Duchessa d'Aosta was a 460 ft long and 60 ft large ship. However the vessel's commander managed, with staggering ease, to turn her to starboard, then to port enabling the ship to break adrift from her anchorage at three knots without the slightest difficulty. The great ship soon sailed past the two buoys marking the entrance to the port, and even overtook the Nuneaton with its two war spoils. The entire operation lasted only 35 minutes without the slightest incident. It was an achievement of extraordinary technical prowess.

On land, the gala dinner had been cut short after the very first explosion. Cars were rushing up and down and there was intense agitation in the port. The second in command of the Italian ship could be seen screaming and gesticulating frantically on the pier. Total confusion reigned throughout.

The return to Lagos was to be more problematic. The Nuneaton broke down only ten miles from Santa Isabel, but fortunately, the SS Ajassa, a British Merchant Navy ship, was there to offer assistance and towed her, together with the other two vessels, into Lagos port. Furthermore, the high sea rendezvous with the warship, HMS Violet did not take place at the planned time, but on the 18th of January at 14.30 hours. However, March-Phillips had the greatest of difficulties in convincing the officer, who had been sent onboard the Vulcan by his Lieutenant-Commander, that he was indeed himself a British officer and that he had just captured the Duchessa d'Aosta. The Royal Navy ship finally escorted the tugboat, together with its spoils, to Lagos, where the Nuneaton and her crew were already waiting. But despite all of these unforeseen and troublesome events, operation Postmaster already appeared to have met with stunning success.

From an economical point of view, the operation transpired to be an excellent manoeuvre. The Italian ship's hold contained wool, copra (dried coconut kernel), coffee and copper, representing a substantial merchant value estimated at more than £250,000.

A few months later, the Royal Navy received orders to transport the vessel to Scotland[6]. From a diplomatic point of view, the British government suffered no prejudice whatsoever from this apparent act of piracy, which, committed on neutral territory, could very well have caused monumental damage, had it met with failure. From a political point of view, the S.O.E had clearly demonstrated its usefulness and efficiency to its many critics in the Foreign Office, the Admiralty, the War Office and the Ministry for Transport. The

[6] *On the 5th of July 1942, the* **Duchessa d'Aosta** *was berthed at James Watt Dock in Greenock (22 miles from Glasgow) under the Union Jack. She was assigned to the Ministry of Fisheries and managed by "Canadian Pacific", renamed:* **Empire Yukon** *and resumed service on the 15th of September 1942. Throughout the rest of the war, she was essentially used for transporting troops. Returned to the Italians in 1947, the ship was finally scrapped in 1952.*

reputation and the prestige of the corps had taken on a whole new dimension. For all of these reasons, the men from the Maid Honor Force were given the warmest and the most enthusiastic of welcomes when they returned to Dorset a few weeks later. The highest military authorities, and in particular their chief, General Gubbins, had made the trip from London to personally congratulate them. They received highly laudatory messages from the Prime Minister's cabinet, from Foreign Affairs and from many other sources. Over the following weeks, all of the men who had taken part in the expedition were congratulated, admired and indulged to such an extent that they were rapt in a feeling of general euphoria.

Military rewards were awarded to those who had particularly distinguished themselves during the operation. On the 22nd of July 1942, as requested by Lord Selbourne, Minister of Economic Warfare, Captain V. Laversuch was named Officer of the Order of the British Empire (OBE)[7]; Captain R.A.J. Lippett and Lieutenant C.A.L. Guise, Members of the Order of the British Empire (MBE); Captain Gustavus March-Phillips was promoted to the grade of Major and decorated

[7] *Created by King George V during the First World War (1917), the* **Order of the British Empire** *comprised five grades, two knighthood grades:* **Knight** *or* **Dame Grand Cross** *(KBE),* **Knight** *or* **Dame Commander** *(KBE), and three further grades:* **Commander** *(CBE),* **Officer** *(OBE) and* **Member** *(MBE).*

[8] *The* **Distinguished Service Order** *was founded by Queen Victoria in 1886 to reward particularly deserving officers, or those who had distinguished themselves throughout active service during the war.*

with the Distinguished Service Order (DSO)[8]; Captain J.G. Appleyard was awarded a silver bar to add to his Military Cross (MC)[9], and finally Lieutenant G. Hayes was awarded with the Military Cross. All of the above distinctions were published in the columns of the very illustrious London Gazette with no citation other than *"in recognition of gallant and distinguished services in the field"*.

A few months prior to the reward ceremony, a reception had been held at the SOE headquarters in Baker Street in honour of the success of the Maid Honor. The entire personnel was invited to celebrate the heroes of operation Postmaster, but also the SOE's entire policy, finally rewarded after so many long months of effort. March-Phillips, blessed at having commanded an exceptionally audacious military action, approached a young woman, Marjorie Marling, a lift service employee at 74 Baker Street. It was love at first site. A month later they were engaged. After their wedding, celebrated on the 18th of April, the couple moved to an unoccupied house in Alford Street[10] belonging to one of Marjorie's cousins.

---

[9] *The **Military Cross** was created on the 28th of December 1915 by George V, in recognition of the bravery of officers during the First World War.*

[10] ***Henrietta March-Phillips**, who was never to know her father, was born in this house. During a radio broadcast in 1971, she evoked the very short-lived bliss of her parents: **"They had a short time together. I can remember my surprise when I realised how short - only 7 months. To me as a child it seemed such a strong thing - I just assumed it must have been much longer".***

Following the tremendous success of his first mission, March-Phillips received permission from General Gubbins to seek headquarters for his commando troop. March-Phillips and Appleyard immediately set out in search of a sufficiently secluded place to be used as a military training ground. They were immediately intrigued by an impressive and apparently uninhabited Elizabethan manor house situated 7 miles from Wareham and 10 miles from Poole and totally isolated in the heart of the Dorset countryside. It seemed to be the ideal spot to accommodate and train their thirty men in a discreet and even charming location, for the manor was surrounded with sumptuous gardens. March-Phillips returned to visit the outstanding 17th Century building with its proprietors, Mr and Mrs Cholmondeleys, who were somewhat uncomfortable at the thought of what this military group might make of their manor house. March-Phillips, who, it turned out, vaguely knew the couple, finally managed to reassure them. Indeed, before the war, he had lived a small distance from Anderson Manor while he was writing Sporting Print at Bere Regis.

Hence, it was at Anderson Manor that Major March-Phillips was to create his new task force. Inspired by his past experience, Gustavus March-Phillips set to developing a new project which he revealed, one day, to his friend Captain Peter Kemp, *"And then he told us his own plan which was to mount*

Anderson Manor

Photograph of the façade of **Anderson Manor** in Dorset. (Photo taken from Anders Lassen, VC, MC, of the SAS by Mike Langley, New English Library, London, 1988).

a series of small raids across the Channel to attack
German strong points, signal stations on the Brittany
coast and the Channel Islands, with the idea of keeping
the Germans, first of all, of scaring them and secondly
causing them to divert more and more troops to
garrison duties to prevent these raids, and in this way
hoped eventually, when he'd been able to mount raids

*A few men from the **Small Scale Raiding Force** in training on the road to Cumberland, summer 1942.*
In the foreground, from left to right: Lord Francis Howard of Penrith, Jack Taylor and Peter O'Rily, pulling the cart, and Graham Hayes smoking his pipe.
In the background: André Desgrange, partly hidden by Lord Howard, and Anders Lassen.

all the length of occupied Europe, from Biarritz up to Norway, that they might have to divert considerable numbers of troops".[11]

March-Phillip's troop was officially known as the 62nd Commando; however its true name, which was

---

[11] Quote from a **BBC** radio broadcast made on the 20th of August 1971.

kept top-secret, became the Small Scale Raiding Force (SSRF) as from the summer of 1942. The troops, who were all ready and willing to take part in raids on enemy territory, gradually became accustomed to life at Anderson Manor, which did not involve particularly strict military discipline. Whilst awaiting his first mission, March-Phillips subjected his troop, which now comprised some 50 men, to intensive day and night training. The commandos were abandoned, in small groups, in isolated locations such as the northern Devon coast. They had to survive on very limited and concentrated rations, using local pond water that they chlorinated to render it drinkable and sleeping in hedges whilst carrying a 48lb backpack.

March-Phillips was convinced that things were finally getting serious when the Royal Navy offered the troop an MTB 344 (Motor Torpedo Boat), a small high-speed experimental vessel. From that time on, the small troop was placed under the control of Combined Operations, and the MTB was to be commanded by Freddie Bourne from the Coastal Forces. The MTB 344 was 60 ft long and propelled by a Thornycroft 1,200 horsepower engine, enabling it to attain a maximum speed of 40 knots[12]. The vessel was also equipped with two further auxiliary engines, one of which was very silent and was destined for use during coastal approach in enemy territory. For sea attacks, it was

---

[12] **Knot**: unit of speed used in maritime navigation and equivalent to 1 nautical mile per hour, or 0,514 metres per second.

equipped with two torpedo launch tubes. Not only was it manoeuvrable, the MTB 344 also had the advantage of being difficult to detect by radar because of its relatively small size. It was armed with two Vickers machine guns, one at each side of the deck, and with Lewis light machine guns to the rear of the bridge. Besides Freddie Bourne, the vessel's initial crew consisted of a navigating officer and seven seamen.

Training of SSRF members therefore included exercises on the "Little Pisser", the affectionate nickname given to the MTB 344 because of the stream of water that could be seen at the rear of the vessel when the engines were on full steam. No time was wasted in preparing the vessel's first mission which was to take place on the night of the 14th of August 1942.

The operation's codename was Barricade. Eleven officers, non-commissioned officers and enlisted men were chosen among the SSRF.

Cast off took place at 20.45 hours from the Hornet base at Portsmouth and an hour later the signal was given for departure from the last buoy situated at the extremity of the NAB channel[13]. The MTB 344 then headed for Barfleur, but shortly after its departure, its main engine started to falter and had to be switched off three times for repair. The MTB finally continued its route with only the starboard engine functioning. At 23.00 hours, the crew could finally distinguish the Barfleur lighthouse. The launch's commander then reduced speed continuing at 18 knots, then at approximately three miles[14] to the east of Barfleur, he cut the main engine and made his approach with the silent auxiliary engine.

The MTB had to repeatedly be brought to a halt in order for the navigator to line up its compass with the Barfleur lighthouse, considerably delaying its arrival. At 01.30 hours the anchor was finally dropped, an hour and a half later than planned. The eleven men were picked up and taken to shore on a small collapsible Goatley boat, a light canvas and wooden-framed craft with four oars and that was far larger than it was deep. After twenty minutes navigation and in total silence, the group set foot, not on the planned shore of "Pointe de Fouli", but three-quarters of a nautical mile further north. The northbound coastal currents of at least two and a half knots had been

[13] The "**NAB channel**" is an access route to guide ships out of, and to a greater extent into Portsmouth harbour. At the channel's extremity, the **Nab Tower**, a small lighthouse emerging from the English Channel marks the beginning of deep sea navigation. The tower was initially attached to a second tower, by means of a chain, in order to prevent enemy submarines from entering into Portsmouth harbour during the First World War. Completed in 1920, the **Nab Tower** has often been mentioned in the operations reports of commanders of vessels berthed in this important naval base. The tower still exists today and, after having undergone several face-lifts in 1983 and 1995 by Trinity House, the official general lighthouse authority responsible for maintaining lighthouses in England, Wales, the Channel Islands and Gibraltar, continues to offer guidance to military and commercial fleets.

[14] **Nautical mile:** 60th part of an equatorial degree (1,852 mètres, 6,080 ft)

Freddie BOURNE

Lieutenant Freddie Bourne,
DSC, RNVR in training aboard an unidentified MTB. Undated (Bourne/Guillou Collection)

▲ *Photograph of the bridge of the MTB 344. From left to right: Lieutenant Russel-Smith, the navigator Rik van Riel, the radio operator Tom Potts and an unidentified sailor. Late 1943. The two swastikas painted on the front of the bridge represent the destruction of two German U-Boats, and the four vertical strokes, the participation in eight commando raids. (Photo taken from The Commandos 1940-1946 by Charles Messenger, William Kimber, London, 1985)* neglected in their estimations. The Goatley was left under the surveillance of a guard, armed with a Thomson submachine gun, while the rest of the group headed off for its target: a detection station and a German anti-aircraft station.

The group left the beach, crossed the fields bordering the coast in single file and penetrated inland. A little later, the column of men came up against a barbed wire fence, which it effortlessly severed, and then a second fence, protecting an important retrenchment, appeared. This second enclosure proved to be far more difficult to cut. Precious time was lost and Major March-Phillips ordered his men to divide into two groups, the first of which was to stay put while the second attempted to bypass the obstruction. The noise caused by the severing of the fencing eventually drew the attention of a sentry who gave the alert. Several German soldiers then left their guard post. When they approached the spot where the commando was hidden, crouching in the obscurity, three plastic bombs were thrown in their direction, producing a terrifying explosion. All of the German soldiers fell prey to machine gunfire from Thomsons and other automatic arms. At least three enemy soldiers were immediately killed and three or four others wounded.

March-Phillips then indicated to his men to regain the beach, which, without difficulty, they located a few minutes later. The surprise effect was a total success. The Germans blindly fired rockets and shot, into the night, in a frenzied and disorderly manner, without entering into pursuit of any genuine target. The land operation had lasted fifty minutes, but the MTB could only be reached half an hour later, at 03.45 hours, again because of currents. During its return journey, two German planes flew over the boat, without making any attempt at attack. At 07.00 hours, Saint Catherine's Point to the south of the Isle of Wight was visible and the harbour entrance was only a few minutes away.

Review of the operation provoked mixed reactions. The predetermined targets were not reached and enemy losses were meagre. However, it had been proven that a few men with an MTB escaping from enemy detection could cause considerable damage on occupied territory. There were no victims among the SSRF troops. It had been demonstrated that a group of a dozen men, specially trained in hit and run attack techniques, was capable of an impact totally out of proportion to its numbers, and therefore appeared to be the ideal task force for such operations. Consequently, the military chiefs' confidence in this special unit was reinforced. These were the main conclusions after the SOE's operation Barricade.

MTB 344 in training in front of the Purbeck
Cliffs, summer 1943. (Photo taken from The
Commandos 1940-1946 by Charles Messenger,
William Kimber, London, 1985)
(All Rights Reserved)

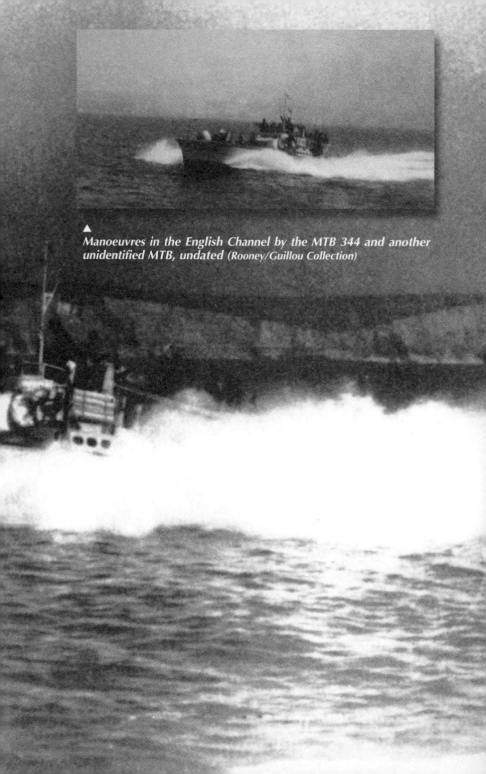

Manoeuvres in the English Channel by the MTB 344 and another unidentified MTB, undated (Rooney/Guillou Collection)

Chapter II
The success of operation *DRYAD*

Aboard the MTB 344, Captain Geoffrey Appleyard knew that this new mission would be nothing like the others for him. Apart from the motorboat's crew members, he was the only man from the SSRF, nominated by March-Phillips to participate in operation Aquatint, who would not disembark.

His ankle pains were a constant reminder of Les Casquets lighthouse raid, ten days previously. His thoughts drifted, for a moment, and he remembered that rock situated to the far north of the Channel Islands and surmounted by a lighthouse whose red light flashed once every fifteen seconds guiding the boat's approach on the night of the 2nd of September 1942.

After innumerable fruitless attempts, abandoned because of bad weather conditions including winds varying from force 3 to force 5, the MTB, commanded by Lieutenant Freddie Bourne, "RNVR" (Royal Navy Volunteer Reserve), finally left Portland Bill on Wednesday 2nd September at 21.00 hours. Despite a very careful overhaul, the port engine proved to be temperamental, and the first 25 miles were therefore covered at a reduced speed of 25 knots.

Aurigny, the most northerly of the Anglo-Norman Isles, was the first to appear, at 22.10 hours at 20° on the port bow, identified by four white lights flashing every five seconds. Appleyard then distinguished two stronger beams of light, on the starboard bow, coming from Guernsey, and a little later he noticed a red vertical signal, again on the port bow, very probably originating from the headland of La Hague at the north-western tip of the Cotentin peninsula.

At 22.45 hours, Les Casquets lighthouse, operation Dryad's target, was clearly identified. Dryad was the official codename given to this new SSRF operation. The MTB's skipper immediately ordered for the main engines to be cut, and the approach was to be made with only the silent auxiliary engine running. At the same time, he changed course in order to approach the target from the north, sailing against the current. Half a mile from the rock, a sailor cast the anchor and the assault group, comprising ten officers and two men, left the MTB to board the Goatley[15] at precisely 00.25 hours.

The landing was made without incident, neither for the men, nor for the vessel, which was already an achievement, for the south-western swell brought strong currents crashing onto the rock. The reefs around Les Casquets had, for a long time, been notorious. Legend has it that shipwrecks were so frequent in the area that the English had taken to recovering cannons. Victor Hugo himself wrote, in "The Channel Archipelago", the opening sequence of his book "The Toilers of the Sea", a few sufficiently eloquent lines on the considerable risks taken by sailors venturing into these perilous waters, *"Les Casquets is a redoubtable place of shipwreck. The English, two hundred years ago, made a business of fishing out the sunken cannons. One of these cannons, covered with oysters and mussels, is in the Valognes Museum."* [16]

---

[15] *A note from the English National Archives (P.R.O., DEFE 2/798) gives details of the "**Characteristics of a "Goatley**" folding boat: 1. 171/2 ft long. 2. c. 5 ft wide (21/2 ft high). 3. Collapses to a height of 9 inches. 4. Expanding of boat: 1½ minutes by 2 men. 5. Every fitting secured to boat except paddles. 6. Can be lifted by 2 or carried by 4 men. 7. Can be launched from deck of destroyer without use of derrick or davits. 8. Wooden bottom and framing covered with rubber. Green canvas material. 9 Paddled by 10 men. 10. Holds 11 men. 11. Weight: 3 cwt (hundredweight). 12. Oblong shape - can go in either direction and can be carried cross country. Very manoeuvrable. Quite a reasonable sea boat. 13. No. 6 Commando had use of them in 1942 and thought that it was the best folding boat that they had been issued with".*

[16] *Translation from **"The Channel Archipelago"**, opening sequence of "The Toilers of the Sea" by Victor Hugo, Nelson Editeurs, Paris, 1955, tome one, page 49.*

Tom WINTER

Aerial photograph of Les Casquets archipelago, undated. (Photo taken from The German Occupation of The Channel Islands by Charles Cruickshank, The Guernsey Press Co. LTD, 1975)

◄ Photograph of Sergeant Tom Winter. On his right sleeve, under the "commando" badge were his parachute licence badge and the Royal Marines commando badge, no place, 1941 (Private collection).

The only men remaining aboard the Goatley were Captain Graham Hayes, expert for all landing missions and the more delicate re-embarkation missions, and another officer, Captain John Burton who kept watch on the front and rear mooring ropes and maintained contact with the MTB via an infrared transmitter.

Under the command of Major March-Phillips, the small troop's first obstacle was the 80 ft high cliff which they had to climb. The clamour of the breakers and the deafening blow of the waves rushing into the caves and crevasses of the rock masked any noise made by the commandos during their ascent. On the clifftop, the group came up against barbed-wire fencing, which was no major hindrance once it had been severed. The south wall of the enclosure was then to be climbed, since the entrance was barricaded with thick barbed wire entanglement. Only a few instants later, the entire group had made its way to the courtyard without being located by the small German garrison occupying the lighthouse and its outbuildings.

At the agreed signal from the Major, the troop split into several groups of two and rushed, some within the lighthouse itself, others throughout the outbuildings: wireless tower, engine room, accommodation and living room. Complete surprise was obtained and all resistance was overcome without a shot being fired. Les Casquets Lighthouse's entire personnel was taken prisoner: seven men, three of whom were young radio operators and three others watchmen, under the orders of the 41 year-old Oberwachtmeister (chief warrant officer). All of the prisoners, including two leading telegraphists who were preparing to go to bed and the two watchmen, were in the accommodation quarters or in the living room. At that precise moment, an amusing event took place; event that was to be recounted after the war with mischievousness by Lord Howard who always liked a joke. One of the Germans who had been surprised in his bed was wearing a hairnet. March-Phillips, who had only glanced at him, thought that Captain Howard was preparing to force a woman out of bed. Before realising his mistake, he ordered Howard to immediately release the prisoner, stuttering a little, as he often did in such unexpected circumstances. Ever since, this comical anecdote is often related in the Anderson Manor mess.

Before leaving, the Major March-Phillips had the wireless sabotaged with axes. However, the light and the engine room were left intact. The buildings and offices were then scrupulously searched for important papers, documents and code books. The harvest proved to be bountiful: a codebook for harbour defence vessels, signal books, records, the wireless telecommunications diary, procedure signals, personal letters and photographs, identity books and passes, ration cards, station log, ration log and a few objects: a gas mask and a gas cape. All of the papers were handed over to the military authorities at Portland on return and were later exploited by various British army departments.

The prisoners, some of whom were still in their nightshirts, were taken to the cliff and climbed down towards the Goatley using the same route as for the commando's ascent. Re-embarkation, which was an extremely delicate operation, took place at 01.00 hours. The 45° slope leading to the Goatley's mooring position had to be slid down by each and every prisoner as and when Corporal Warren gave them the go-ahead. They then had to be hoisted onboard as soon as the swell brought the vessel to the desired level. In his operation report, March-Phillips stressed the perilousness of this particular episode, and congratulated his men in charge of re-embarkation: *"Great credit is due to all concerned that this operation was successful, for one mistake might have meant the swamping of the boat, which might have brought disaster on the party"*.[17]

The Casquet Lighthouse's garrison was equipped with a relatively small quantity of arms and ammunition. Each man was equipped with a rifle of the old Steyr pattern and there were two large cases of stick grenades as well as an Oerlikon Cannon-Shell, small calibre gun. However the Major did stress the following, *"If a good watch had been kept, or if any loud noises had been made on the approach or on landing, the rock could have been rendered pretty well impregnable by seven determined men"*.[18] With

[17] Public Record Office, Kew, Operation **Dryad**, operation report by Major G. March-Phillips, 9th September 1942, page 22.

[18] Idem, page 22.

regards to the arms found on site, he added the following comment, which transpires to be somewhat disconcerting when considering his tragic destiny and that of two of his men, *"Particular attention is called to the presence of stick grenades in such outposts, for they are formidable weapons".[19]*

At 01.10 hours, all of the commando members, together with their prisoners: a total of 19 men, were safely embarked on the Goatley. Operation Dryad was completed in less than an hour; record timing. The only unfortunate incidents were Captain Kemp's leg injury unintentionally caused by one of his comrade's daggers, and Captain Appleyard's ankle which was twisted during re-embarkation. Appleyard was the last to board the Goatley, having remained on the slippery rock to maintain the vessel in place. He had to jump onboard after having released the last mooring rope. At this stage, the Goatley had already distanced itself from its mooring point and Appleyard's foot hit the deck somewhat precariously, twisting his ankle.

To lighten the Goatley's burden, March-Phillips ordered for the arms collected at the lighthouse to be thrown overboard. Still heavily laden, the vessel rode the swell admirably. Before receiving the signal to approach, the MTB's commander, Freddie Bourne, decided to weigh the anchor which was dragging the boat northwards, thus enabling the transfer to be made

---

[19] *Ibidem, page 22.*

at 01.35 hours, only 500 metres from Les Casquets rock.

According to the operation report, the seven prisoners proved to be "very docile" and they were battened down in the forecastle with Captain Dudgeon and two other crew members. The voyage home, although in an increasingly rising sea, was without mishap and the MTB docked at Portland at 04.00 hours.

The mission was a complete success: rapid execution, a wireless station put out of action, seven German prisoners who, together with the collected papers, were to offer precious information.[20] No victims, no material damage. Major March-Phillips concluded in his report: *"Great credit is due to Lieutenant Bourne for his handling of the ship in this and the previous operation, both of which were hazardous and difficult undertakings in close proximity to reefs and sunken rocks, and to Captain Appleyard, whose navigation made them possible. Also to Private*

---

[20] **Report n° 5062 by Gustavus March-Phillips** *includes an appendix "D" of several pages indicating, over and above the identity, grade, origin and career of the German officers taken prisoner, further information of indiscutable military value on the positions they had occupied at Les Casquets Lighthouse: the Cherbourg listening post, the anti-air defence and the Fort West beacon "Hafenkommandantur", the Cap de La Hague Lighthouse, the Pointe de Barfleur Lighthouse, the Marine Flak Regiment 20 in the Lorient district. The report's precision was such that the British secret services even knew which bars the soldiers regularly visited during leave in Cherbourg.*

Orr, a German speaker, who marshalled the prisoners and did much to make the search successful".[21]

All of the details of operation Dryad were still fresh in Geoffrey Appelyard's memory, and if only his wretched ankle weren't to prevent him from landing with his friend Gus on the Normandy beach a few instants later, everything would be just fine.

---

[21] *Ibidem, page 23.*

CHAPTER III
THE MEN FROM OPERATION
AQUATINT

Appleyard the left bridge of the MTB 344 to exchange a few words with the other members of the commando at the rear of the vessel.

In the obscurity, he had trouble distinguishing the tense faces of the small troop, but he immediately recognised the slender silhouette of his old friend Graham Hayes and sat down beside him. Words were superfluous; the friendship between the two men was evident at a simple glance. What could have been Graham's thoughts at that precise instant; his parents perhaps, who lived in the same town as the Appleyards, in Linton-on-Wharfe?

Geoffrey's mind was filled with fond memories of cherished places. First of all, Kiln Hill, Mr and Mrs Hayes' residence in Linton. Geoffrey could still clearly remember his mother's alarmed expression and his father's simultaneous amusement when Mr and Mrs

H.C. Hayes informed them that their second son had just signed up as a sailor on a Finish sailing boat, the Pommern, owned by the rich Finish ship-owner Gustaf Adolf Erikson. At the time, in 1939, this grand four-mast bark was making its last worldwide race: the Australian Grain Race, a famous boat race from Australia to England opposing sailing boats, laden with grain.[22]

He also remembered Wetherby, the closest town to Linton, where he would watch Graham training with the local Rugby Union Football Club, just before the war. Graham's finesse and his excellent team spirit made him extremely popular.

[22] *Built in 1903 in the **Hamburg shipyards** for the German firm B. Wencke & Son, the **Pommern** was initially called the Mneme, an abbreviation of Mnemosyn, the Greek goddess of memory. She was used as a merchant ship by her German owners and sailed across Europe and South America. After the First World War, the **Pommern**, considered as a war spoil, was allotted to the Greeks. Put up for sale in 1923, she was bought by the Finish ship-owner Gustaf Erikson who had the ship used to transport grain between Spencer, in Australia and various ports in England and Ireland. In 1939, the **Pommern** made her final journey from Hull (Kingston upon Hull) in the Humber Estuary to Mariehamn, her home port in the Ahvenanmaa Aland Islands in Finland. Graham Hayes had enrolled for this ultimate journey, and arrived in the port just before the beginning of the Second World War. Having survived the war, this 310 ft long boat, whose total sail surface was of almost 35,000 square feet, was given in offering to the town of Mariehamn by Gustaf Erikson's children in 1952-53. Since restored, thanks to the former sailors association Cap Horniers, she has been converted into a **floating museum.***

Graham HAYES

Portrait of **Graham Hayes** before the war, no place, no date.
(Private collection)

Temple Sowerby, a small town situated in Cumberland, was where Graham had set up his wood sculpture studio in 1938, after having been apprentice to the Kilburn sculptor, Robert Thomson who everyone nicknamed "The Mouseman", because of the small rodent he always carried with him. Perhaps it was this whimsical master who led Graham, himself, to take on the taming of an old crow. In any case, he was famous in the local pub where he regularly took Grip, his domesticated bird, perched on his shoulder. Geoffrey could remember seeing a photograph of Graham and his crow posing in front of the pub. The apprentice sculptor was also proud to show off his first works of art that he was eager to sell, but the declaration of war was to put a stop to those plans.

Finally, Geoffrey recalled, as if it were happening again before his very eyes, this last memory: Graham had just learned in August that he had been awarded the illustrious Military Cross for his admirable attitude during the Fernando Po mission. What a tremendous souvenir! Graham was radiant. The entire SSRF team had organised a splendid evening party for him in the officers' mess at Anderson Manor. A discreet smile appeased, for a few seconds, Geoffrey's tense expression.

Seated on Graham's other side was Francis, or rather Lord Francis Howard of Penrith. Before distin-guishing his fine long features, Geoffrey immediately recognised his' voice. Geoffrey was familiar with Francis' experience before joining the SSRF. He was much older than Geoffrey, who, at 26, was the youngest officer, or than Graham who was only 29. At the age of nearly 38, Francis was in fact one of the most "elderly" members of the SSRF.

One day, at Anderson Manor, just after a training session on the Dorset beaches close to Lulworth Cove, Captain Howard had told Geoffrey the story of his childhood. Francis Howard was born in the Chigi Palace in Rome in 1905. He was the second of five children, all boys, and his father, Esmé William Howard was a distinguished diplomat. After having been attached to the British Embassy in Rome, he was named Consul General of Crete, before occupying several positions in Hungary, Switzerland and Sweden. He finally concluded his career as British Ambassador in Washington from 1924 to 1930, ennobled by King George V with the title of Lord Howard of Penrith.

Francis' mother, Isabella Giustiani-Bandini, was the sixth daughter of Prince Giustiniani-Bandini, Duke of Mondragone and 8th Earl of Newburgh, from an ancient Italian family whose ancestors had even been papal bankers.

Francis followed his parents and, from country to country, his father's various consular transfers. His education began with private tuition in Stockholm, after which he was schooled, for a number of years, at the eminent Trinity College, Cambridge. His parents were keen for him to study law, but Francis' free time and school holidays were spent satisfying his passion for literature in the company of Proust, Gibbon and many other great masters. Thanks to a scholarship, Francis was accepted at the prestigious Harvard Law School and, in 1927, he got his first job in a prominent Wall Street investment firm "J.P. Morgan & Co". He was therefore able to keep in touch with his parents who were still in Washington. But Francis' greatest memory of the pre-war period, was, without a doubt, the extraordinary six month journey in the West Indies with his father, part of which was onboard a private train.

On his return to England, he continued his law studies and, from 1932, he worked in a renowned Middle Temple law firm specialised in estate adminis-tration. Francis became a close friend of his boss Arthur Cole, a highly cultivated and noted bibliophile. He also acted as a legal aid lawyer at Tynbee Hall in the East End of London.

On the 1st of August 1939, his father died at the age of 75. Having lost his elder brother in 1926, Francis therefore inherited the peerage and, thus, the SSRF contained, among its members, a genuine English Lord. When war was declared, Francis Howard signed up as a private in the first army unit he came across. However, one of Her Majesty's Lords could not conceivably remain at this level and he was rapidly promoted to the rank of Captain of an anti-aircraft

Lord Francis HOWARD OF PENRITH

Captain Lord Howard of Penrith with a few of his SSRF comrades, in training on the road to Cumberland in the north-west of England. Summer 1942.

battery. Captain Howard, who dreamed of adventure, found this position to be increasingly dull, and he seized the opportunity to enlist in the newly formed 62ⁿᵈ Commando, thus joining Major March-Phillips on his return from Africa. His presence has already been mentioned during operation Dryad on Les Casquets Lighthouse.

Geoffrey knew that Francis Howard was not yet married, but that he was engaged to Anne Bazley, née Hotham, widowed in 1934; they had promised each other that they would marry before the end of the war.

Because of the noise of the MTB's engine, Geoffrey didn't quite seize what Francis Howard had said to Lieutenant Tony Hall. He knew very little of this officer. Silently, he observed this relatively tall man, of a height of around 5'11", who was always cheerful and amusing. What Geoffrey did know was that Tony was a "bon-vivant" and his appreciation of the good things in life had already taken him to Normandy and Brittany on a gastronomical bicycle tour with an American friend. His gourmet palate had been enchanted by almost every traditional Breton and Norman speciality, with the exception of the "Tripes à la mode de Caen"… It was very probably for the same reason that he enjoyed the company of Francis Howard who himself revelled in a good joke or a witty remark. Geoffrey had often discovered the two men discussing historical events. Could this have been provocation on Tony's part? The French constable Bertrand Du Guesclin who, during the Hundred Years' War, had "thrown the English out of France", had become his favourite historical hero.

Gus had told Geoffrey that Hall had started his military career as a private in the Irish Guards, one of the regiments also known as the London Irish and in charge of the protection of the Royal Family at Buckingham Palace. That's why he wore a kilt, even during his private outings in London. Tony Hall had been promoted to the rank of Sergeant and had travelled to Norway and Sweden. He had studied in Sweden and had even worked for a while as a lumberjack. The army had chosen him to take part, as a civilian, in a special operation in Finland, but the mission had failed.

After having left the army, he launched himself into a radio career, and since he proved to be talented, he met with considerable success, particularly as a script-writer. He took part in the production of several radio programmes such as: "Danger Men at Work" or "In Town Tonight". He also wrote several articles for the humoristic magazine Punch, among others.

Upon the declaration of war, he enlisted again and was assigned to military intelligence. He had applied to join the 62nd Commando and impressed the jury with his eagerness and his linguistic skills to such an extent that, despite a negative medical exam due to his poor sight, he finally obtained the recruitment commission's approval.

Tony HALL

▲
On the left, **Tony Hall** in his Irish
Guards Lieutenant's uniform in the
streets of London, undated.
(Private collection)

Portrait of ▶
Tony Hall
before the war.
No place,
no date.
(Private collection)

Further away, Geoffrey could see John Burton talking to the Frenchman André Desgrange. Geoffrey only knew Captain Burton since his enlistment in the SSRF. He took part in operation Dryad and Geoffrey had appreciated his self-control and his perfect manoeuvring skills during the embarkation of the German prisoners.

Maître Desgrange was the only officer among the foreign members of the SSRF. He was part of the Maid Honor Force and therefore one of the troop's oldest members. Geoffrey made acquaintance with him on the liner that was to take them to Freetown late August 1941. He remembered him, there in Africa, when the troop was impatiently waiting for the go ahead for operation Postmaster.

André Desgrange's background was probably the most original of the entire commando. Born on the 19th of February 1911 at Baume-les-Dames (in the Doubs region of France), André Desgrange started work at the early age of 14 at the "Fonderies de Sainte-Suzanne", iron foundry in the region of Montbéliard, before working in the Peugeot factory in Sochaux. At the age of 19, he joined the French Navy in Toulon. In 1940, he managed to make his way to England and joined the Free French Naval Force (F.N.F.L.). He was given the rank of boatswain, in other words, of officer risen from the ranks, however, his relative inactivity was a burden to him. He had heard about the recent creation of a special commando the British Army's within Combined Operations and decided to apply. When he stood before the recruitment commission, his singular experience, his ardent desire to fight off the enemy, as well as his physical endurance capacities all led to him being readily accepted within Major March-Phillips' small training group.

At the other side of the rear deck, with his back to Geoffrey, Sergeant Tom Winter was holding onto the bulwark rail and talking to sergeant Alan Williams. There was a significant age difference between the two men. Tom was already 37, just like Francis Howard, whilst Alan only admitted to being 22, which made him, by far, the youngest member of the team. Geoffrey had already noticed that Tom had taken Alan, who had been recruited mainly for his physical combat skills, under his wing. Sergeant Thomas Winter was from the Royal Army Service Corps. He had been awarded his Sergeant's stripes there, and had then applied to join the Commandos. Tom wasn't of an exceptional corpulence. He was in fact rather small and of somewhat frail features. But this first impression turned out to be misleading for he was extraordinarily supple and proved to be of surprising muscular strength. His strong personality could lead him to be inflexible during service, and he knew how to easily obtain respect and obedience from his men. However, underneath this apparently rough nature, Tom Winter could also be the most charming of men. Major March-Phillips immediately saw in him a valuable man, perfectly suitable for special commando type missions. Without hesitating, he had chosen him to take part in operation Postmaster on the island of Fernando Po. Geoffrey knew that Tom, together with Graham Hayes, had distinguished himself during the capture of the Likomba and the Bibundi, by his remarkable physical skills and sense of initiative. He had also demonstrated his great efficiency and perfect self-confidence in the transmission and execution of orders during operation Dryad.

Alan Williams' first military experience was in a Queen's Royal Regiment unit. Operation Aquatint[23] was his first real commando mission. So Tom Winter, who had sensed the anxiety that had been knawing at Alan since their departure, tried to reassure him.

Next to them, three of the four foreigners had chosen to cross the Channel together, slightly isolated from the other team members. Geoffrey knew little of them. Within the SSRF, disciplinary respect and military rules were not given the same consideration as in regular army units. The same applied to differences in rank. At Anderson Manor, all men were treated as equals. As far as March-Phillips was concerned, only their true value

---

[23] *The code name given to this operation does not appear to have any particular significance. It corresponds to the French word* **"aquatinte"** *meaning an acid engraving technique imitating wash-drawing.*

was important. However, despite that, a private remains a private and Jan Hellings, Richard Lehniger and Abraham Opoczynski didn't feel particularly comfortable with the officers. Their integration was troubled further by their language difficulties. Although the three men spoke a limited amount of English, they preferred to converse together in German.

Jan Hellings' military experience before joining March-Phillips' team at Anderson Manor is unfortunately unknown to us. However, it is reasonable to suppose that he enlisted in a regular British army unit, just like the Czech, Richard Lehniger and the Pole, Abraham Opoczynski, before joining the N°10 Commando, comprised of Frenchmen, Dutchmen and Belgians, or the N°2 Commando, comprising Dutch volunteers from the end of March 1942.

Richard Lehniger was the oldest of the three men. He was born on the 9th of June 1900 in Petschau[24], in Bohemia. At the time, the town of Petschau was part of the Austro-Hungarian Empire and was situated 14 miles from the famous northern Bohemian thermal town of Karlsbad[25]. Richard was the eldest of four children from a modest family and spent his childhood in Eger[26], a town situated on the Sudeten border

---

[24] **Petschau** was renamed **Becov Nad Teplou** by the Czechs after the war.

[25] **Karlsbad was renamed: Karlovy Vary.**

[26] **Eger** is now called **Cheb.**

between Karlsbad and the German town of Beyreuth. His father, Gustav, was a barber and his mother Gisèla, née Buxbaum, the third of a Jewish family of twelve children, was originally from Berlin. Gisèla had accepted to marry Gustav, who was not a Jew, at the Lutheran church in Bohemia. Richard's father had fought during the First World War and died in 1916 from wounds received on the front lines. At a very young age, Richard therefore became the main source of support for his mother and his three sisters. However, in 1917, he decided to enlist in the Austrian army and fought on the Italian front until the end of the war. When he was demobilised, he worked as a roofer and church steeple repairman.

One of the main reasons behind Lehniger's entry into the commando was his athletic aptitude; he was an excellent skier and loved climbing.

Richard lost his job during the economical crisis in 1930 and went back to studying economical and political science at Prague University. As a member of the Czech Communist Party, he played an active role in the student unrest during which he met his wife, Julia Dörfler who presided the social democratic student union in Prague. Born in 1914, she was far younger than Richard, but shared his interest in political action. Despite their differing opinions, their common desire to fight the Nazi ideology that had recently triumphed in Germany and their opposition to the ever-threatening risk of war had drawn them closer together.

They both found themselves in an extremely vulnerable position when Bohemia was annexed by Hitler in March 1939. Richard, who was the more exposed of the two, due to his communist activities and his Jewish origins, immediately left Czechoslovachia for Norway. Julia was only able to emigrate on the 17th of August 1939, despite the fact that she had obtained a visa from the British authorities in May. They had planned to leave for Canada and to set up a farm there on virgin land. As soon as Richard learned that his fiancée had left Czechoslovachia for England, he joined her on the 29th of August and they planned to marry before setting off for Canada. However, the declaration of war was to disrupt their plans.

The wedding did, however, take place on the 15th of November 1939, in Margate, in Kent. Richard could very well have chosen to stay, peacefully, in England, but his hatred for Nazism was such that his acts needed to be in line with his convictions. He needed to fight, arms in hand, the new Hitlerian order that had brought Poland to its knees in only a few weeks. Three months before their daughter Irene's birth in late June 1940, he joined the British Army. Like many other Czechs who signed up at the time, Richard Lehniger was assigned to the N° 93 Company of the Auxiliary Military Pioneer Corps (A.M.P.C.), a non-combatant military unit comprising around 280 Central European refugees most of whom were recruited in October 1939 at Kitchener camp in Richborough, Kent. Together with three other companies, all commanded by British officers, N° 93 Company was in charge of laborious excavation work such as the construction of roads, camps and defence and anti-air shelters. At the very beginning of the war, the AMPC was sent to France with the British Expeditionary Force (BEF). On the 11th of May 1940, Richard Lehniger arrived at Le Havre with his Group Pioneer Corps unit which was immediately assigned the task of road construction. He was later sent to a railway warehouse in the vicinity of Beaumont-Le-Roger (Eure region). On the 23rd of May, N° 93 Company received guns and ammunition and, because of the advancing German troops, they made their way to Saint-Malo from where they embarked on the 15th of June for Southampton. The Company was immediately disarmed upon its arrival in England. At the time, the British Army did not apparently have total confidence in all of its foreign troops.

The unit was then dispersed throughout Great Britain, certain troops being sent to Devon and Somerset in the West, others, among whom Richard Lehniger, being sent to Scotland. Lehniger was eager to serve in a fighting unit and, as soon as it was possible for him to do so, he volunteered to join the Commandos. It was hence that, after tough and intensive training at the later renowned Achnacarry training school, Richard Lehniger was very probably assigned to N° 10 Commando, in the N° 3 Troop, comprising mainly Germans, Austrians and Czechs.

Richard Lehniger was one of the last men to join March-Phillips' SSRF troop. Over and above his strong ideological inspiration, his excellent physical skills and his perfect command of the German language; his military experience, including an active role in operation Jubilee in Dieppe[27] on the 19th of August 1942, was to win the jury's confidence. Since that raid, Geoffrey knew that Richard was known as "Richard Leonard", hiding his true identity because of his legitimate fear of the rapid discovery of his Jewish origins in the case of capture by the Germans.

[27] **On the 19th of August 1942**, an allied force, under the orders of General Roberts and Captain Hallet, comprising 5,000 Canadians, 1,100 Brits and 50 American rangers scattered, as observers, among a number of units, landed on an eleven mile long stretch of coastline on either side of **Dieppe harbour**. For **Lord Mountbatten**, Commander of Combined Operations, the exercise was aimed at testing German defences when faced with a landing operation. The operation's success depended on its surprise effect and speed and efficiency were therefore essential. Nine hours after having set foot on the beaches, the commando was decimated and had no choice but to opt for emergency re-embarkation, under violent enemy fire, whilst leaving behind substantial equipment and supplies.

Operation **Jubilee** ended in a terrible defeat with immense human losses: over 4,000 troops out of combat: 667 killed, 218 missing and 1,894 prisoners among the Canadian troops alone.

As far as equipment was concerned, the Royal Navy had lost 33 landing barges and a destroyer; the Army had lost 27 tanks and the Royal Air Force, in charge of aerial cover had lost 106 of its aircraft.

However, the operation was to offer several lessons to the Allies: all landing operations should be preceded by massive aerial and naval preparation; they should cover, a far longer front line, the operation's date should be kept absolutely secret - this was not the case for Dieppe; and finally, landing in well defended ports should be avoided, hence **Winston Churchill's** decision, on Lord Louis Mountbatten's recommendations, to build **artificial ports**.

Richard LEHNIGER

Richard Lehniger, in his **Pioneer Corps** uniform, is in the centre of this photograph between his cousin Léo Félix (on his right) and a comrade (on his left), no place, no date (c. 1941-1942). (Private collection)

◄ *Richard Lehniger*, in his Austrian Army uniform. Photograph taken in 1917 in R. Jugt's professional photography studio. (Private collection)

We also have little knowledge of the Pole Abraham Opoczynski's story; however his motives were similar to those of the other foreign members of the SSRF. After having left his homeland, conquered and occupied by the Germans, in September 1939, he managed to make his way to England and to enlist in the British army to fight against Nazism. He was initially assigned to a royal regiment, the Queen's Own in the west of Kent. When he was accepted into the Commandos, he received the order, for security's sake, to call himself "Adam Orr". His parents, Hirsh and Yetta Opoczynski had stayed in Poland, however L. Spiro, his half-brother on his mother's side, who lived in Forest Gate in Essex, was to be of precious help to him since his arrival in England.

This was not Abraham Opoczynski's first SSRF mission on enemy territory, since he had already taken part in operation Dryad on Les Casquets Lighthouse. Major March-Phillips distinguished him at the very end of his operation report, with the following praise, *"Credit is also due to Private Orr, a German speaker, who marshalled the prisoners and did much to make the search successful"*. However, just like Sergeant Williams, Orr had great difficulty in concealing his apprehension as the MTB approached the French coastline.

Part two:

CODENAME
AQUATINT

CHAPTER I
THE GERMAN DEFENCE SYSTEM

By the end of 1942, the Germans had barely commenced work on the formidable defence system that was to be known as the "Atlantic Wall" (Atlantikwall). However, they had already taken a number of military and civilian measures to ensure the protection of the coast against enemy attacks, be they hit and run missions or major landing operations, like operation Jubilee on Dieppe on the 19th of August 1942.

As from the 20th of October 1942, the Feldkommandantur 723 in Caen had declared a "prohibited coastal zone" covering a 10 to 15 mile deep strip of land stretching, from west to east, from the Cherbourg - Caen primary road via Bayeux, to the Caen - Pont-L'Evêque primary road via Troarn and Dozulé. Only Calvados residents able to provide written proof of their main place of abode, provided by their local Mayor, were allowed to penetrate into this zone. Any other civilians wishing to access the zone could only do so with special permission delivered by the German authorities.

In Saint-Laurent-sur-Mer, as in Vierville-sur-Mer, and many other coastal resorts, the Germans had forbidden access to many villas which were holiday homes to Parisians and therefore only occupied a few months a year. As indicated on a certificate delivered by the Mayor of Vierville-sur-Mer on the 3rd of April 1942, several villas were requisitioned by soldiers from the Wehrmacht or the Luftwaffe who were stationed in the area. At that date, nine villas were already occupied by three officers and approximately 90 non-commissioned officers and troops, and sixteen other villas were kept available to accommodate up to 200 German soldiers if necessary.

The locals were still allowed to visit limited sectors of the beaches at certain hours of the day and they informed many villa owners of deterioration or theft on their property. Complaints flooded into the local village council offices and were forwarded to the Sub-prefecture in Bayeux. However, the grievances passed on by the Sub-Prefect Rochat to Major Hoffmann, Commander of the Kreiskommandantur 789 in Bayeux were, more often than not, totally futile.

At the end of 1941, German military strategy was significantly modified following the United States' entrance into war. From an initially offensive stance, the Germans adopted a defensive position, following

▲
View of the Saint-Laurent-sur-Mer coast before the war. Postcard.
(Private collection)

▲
View of the beach at Saint-Laurent-sur-Mer before the war. Postcard.
(Private collection)

Hitler's directive in December 1941 giving orders to build a line of defence across the western European coastline. In June 1941, the supreme command of the western front, covering some 4,000 kilometres of coastline stretching from the south-west of France to the north of Norway, was given to Field-Marshal Von Witzleben.

At the time, the Todt Organisation's[28] responsibility was limited to defending major ports such as Le Havre and Cherbourg in Normandy; to building large concrete shelters for U-boats on the Atlantic coast: Brest, Lorient, Saint-Nazaire, La Pallice and Bordeaux, and in other strategic zones such as the Pas-de-Calais coastline where 12,000 labourers were employed to erect five heavy artillery emplacements.

The genuine starting point of the Atlantikwall, (the "Atlantic Wall"), was Hitler's directive n°40 (Die Weisung n° 40) on the 23rd of March 1942 entitled:

---

[28] *Created in 1938, the Todt Organisation was named after its originator,* **Fritz Todt**, *a German General and technician and one of the Nazi party's very first militants (1922). Todt had already demonstrated his skill and efficiency by building, from 1933, over 3,700 miles of auto bahn, and by erecting the* **Westwall** *on the French border* **(the West Wall or Siegfried Line)**. *Accumulating honours and new positions:* **Major General** *of the Luftwaffe (1939), Reich Minister for Armaments and Munitions (1940), Inspector General in the Four Year Plan, Chief Administrator in all fields of construction, General Inspector for hydraulic/electrical engineering, Fritz Todt enjoyed great prestige and even the personal admiration of the Führer himself. He was* **killed when his plane crashed**, *near Rastenburg in East Prussia on the 8th of February 1942.*

Küstenverteidigung (coastal defence). It stated his European defence policy and detailed its organisation, specifying the powers of command and the assignations given to each of his three arms of service.

In directive n°41, given on the 13th of August 1942, Hitler entrusted the Todt Organisation with the construction of the wall that was to shelter the Germans from any exterior aggression along the French, Belgian and Dutch coastline. To provide such protection, the Atlantic coast, from the English Channel to the North Sea, was to be adorned with 15,000 concrete blockhouses whose construction was to be completed before the 1st of May 1943.

THE GENERAL ORGANISATION

Three defensive structures were created along the coastline: the Verteidigungsbereiche, or "Defence sector"; the Stützpunkt or "Strong point" and the Widerstandnest or "Resistance nest".

The "Defensive" sector, in charge of the protection of harbours and river estuaries, comprised powerful defence arms from small artillery and Flak (Flugzeugabwehrkanone or anti-aircraft gun) to heavy calibre artillery.

The "Strong point" comprised several small shelters housing Pak antitank guns (Panzerabwehr-kanone), machine-guns and search lights, all protected with barbed-wire fencing and mines. As an autonomous defence position, the base included three or four "Resistance nests", each of which was guarded by a section.

The "resistance nests" were surveillance posts, comprising a few light arms, generally machine-guns, placed within a concrete niche (tobruk), together with a few combat positions linked by trenches. They were the Wehrmacht's smallest defence installations and were designed to watch over a lighthouse, a cove or a small coastal zone.

THE COMMAND

The ground Army (das Heer) was responsible for the greatest part of coastal defence. The area to the centre and the north-west of Calvados was the responsibility of the 716th Infantry Division, under the orders of General Matterstock[29]. The command post was situated in Caen in Rue Leverrier and Avenue de Bagatelle. The division was part of the LXXXIV Army-Corps commanded by General Behlendorff[30], whose headquarters was in Saint-Lô, and who ultimately reported to the 7th Army commanded by General Friedrich Dollmann[31] in his headquarters in Rue Chanzy in the town of Le Mans.

At the lower end of the division's hierarchy, the Saint-Laurent-sur-Mer sector was controlled by the 726th Infantry Regiment, commanded by 47 year-old

[29] General **Otto Matterstock** was born in Karbach on the 19th of October 1889. He enlisted on the 19th of July 1909, was promoted to the rank of Second Lieutenant on the 15th of December 1911 and assigned to the Bavarian 17th Infantry Regiment. He was demobilised after the end of the First World War on the 27th of April 1920, then began a career in the Land of Bavaria police which he later left on the 15th of October 1935 to join the Wehrmacht with the rank of Lieutenant. Rapidly climbing the military ranks, he was promoted to Colonel on the 1st of January 1937 and commanded Würzburg for a short period, from the 1st of June 1938 to the 1st of September 1939. Initially assigned to the 73rd Infantry Regiment, he took command of the 330th Infantry Regiment on the 1st of December 1939. On the 3rd of May 1941, he was named Commander of the 716th Infantry Division whose headquarters were in Caen. On the 1st of September 1941, he was again promoted to the rank of General **(Generalmajor)** in charge of defence on the Normandy coastline between the River Dives and the Vire. He was to be replaced on the 1st of April 1943 by General Wilhelm Richter.

[30] General of Artillery **Hans Behlendorff** was born on the 13th of August 1889 in Allenstein. A First World War veteran, Behlendorff joined the Wehrmacht in 1935 and became General **(Generalmajor)** on the 1st of March 1938. He took command of the 34st Infantry Division on the 19th of July 1939. He was promoted to the rank of Lieutenant General **(Generalleutnant)** on the 1st of February 1940, and was seriously wounded on the 10th of May 1940 on the western front. He was named Commander of the LX Army-Corps on the 15th of December 1941, and transferred on the 25th of May 1942 to the LXXXIV Army-Corps in Saint-Lô under the orders of General Friedrich Dollmann. On the 1st of April 1943, he was placed in reserve at the Wehrmacht High Command and on the 1st of August 1943, he was replaced by General Erich Marcks.

[31] **Friedrich Dollmann** was born on the 2nd of February 1882 in Würzburg. Enlisted in 1899, within the Bavarian 7th Artillery Regiment, he commanded an artillery battalion during the First World War. On the 1st of October 1939, he was named Commander of the German 7th Army which he led in the invasion of France in May and June 1940. He was promoted to the rank of Colonel-General **(Generaloberst)** on the 19th of July 1940 and continued his mission to defend Brittany and western Normandy.

Colonel Münstermann whose headquarters were in Bayeux. Under his command was Battalion Major Hans Grote, aged 51, who commanded the 2nd and 3rd Reserve Infantry Regiments at Saint-Laurent-sur-Mer. This battalion was in charge of the "group of strong points" (Stützpunktgruppe) situated along the coastline, either on the beaches or slightly inland on dominating heights.

A company protected each "strong point" (Stützpunkt). This was the very basis, and the most frequent of German coastal defence systems.

THE COASTAL SECTOR OF SAINT-LAURENT-SUR-MER/VIERVILLE-SUR-MER

The coastal sector of Saint-Laurent-sur-Mer was thus protected in September 1942 by six "strong points": Stützpunktes 27, 28 and 29, commanded by Chief Warrant Officer Pie, at Saint-Laurent-sur-Mer and Stützpunktes 30, 31 and 32, at Vierville-sur-Mer. The same structure repeated itself throughout the Calvados coastline.

Stützpunkt 29 was located on the spot where the Commando was preparing to land and comprised three "resistance nests" (Widerstandsneste, or W.N.): W.N. 29a, W.N. 29b and W.N. 29c.

The manning and the arms on W.N.s varied, but thanks to German reports drafted immediately after operation Aquatint, we have precise knowledge of those on Stützpunkt 29. W.N. 29a was located 220 yards from the beach at Saint-Laurent-sur-Mer which it dominated from a height of 80 to 100 feet above sea level. A marshy zone situated between the beach and W.N. 29a naturally reinforced its position. Defence strength was twenty-seven men including three non-commissioned officers, nineteen men from the Wehrmacht and, quite surprisingly, a non-commissioned officer and four men from the Luftwaffe. The group's arms included seventeen rifles, two heavy machine guns, two 9 mm Schmeisser 40 submachine guns, eight 9mm P 08 guns and two heavy grenade launchers.

W.N. 29b was located on the beach 275 yards to the west. Like all W.N.s, it was protected by barbed-wire fencing and was manned by two non-commissioned officers and nine soldiers. Their arms included seven rifles, a light machine gun, a submachine gun, two P 08 guns and a flamethrower.

W.N. 29c was located, again on the beach, 165 yards farther west. It was manned by a non-commissioned officer and thirteen soldiers armed with twelve rifles, a light machine gun, a heavy machine gun, two P 08 guns, a flamethrower and a 75 mm anti-tank gun. The gun, just like those situated on Stützpunktes 30 and 32, had not yet been protected by a tobruk in the summer of 1942.

Every night, regular patrols ensured continuous contact between the Stützpunkt's different W.N.s, and the night of the 12th of September 1942 was no different.

Patrol n°1, from the 3rd Reserve Company of the 726th Infantry Regiment had been designated on the duty roster to maintain contact between the three W.N.s of Stützpunkt 29. The patrol was commanded by Corporal Wichert and included a further four infantrymen, each armed with a rifle and four hand grenades. Corporal Wichert carried a submachine gun and one of his men, Private Kowalski, was more heavily armed with a light machine gun and was accompanied by a guard dog which he held on leash.

The patrol left the village of Saint-Laurent-sur-Mer and followed the coast, passing by W.N. 28b then crossing the marshy zone just below W.N. 29a. Corporal Wichert had the impression that everything was peaceful on that obscure cloudy night. The sea was calm and the wind moderate. It was precisely 02.00 hours on the Corporal's watch and the slow movement of the ebbing tide had already begun. He noticed that the sea was already 15 feet from the beach. In a few minutes, his patrol would reach W.N. 29b, while patrol n°2, comprising a corporal and five men, was heading from W.N. 30a towards W.N. 29c (cf. map of the raid drafted by the Germans on the 13th of September 1942 at 02.00 hours, page 106).

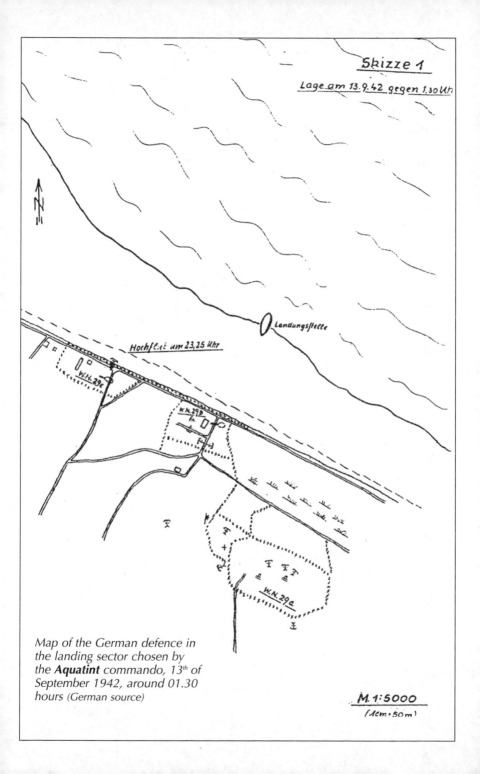

Skizze 1

Lage am 13.9.42 gegen 1,30 Uhr

Landungsstelle

Hochflut um 23,25 Uhr

W.N. 29c

W.N. 29b

W.N. 29a

N

Map of the German defence in
the landing sector chosen by
the **Aquatint** commando, 13th of
September 1942, around 01.30
hours (German source)

M 1:5000
(1cm = 50 m)

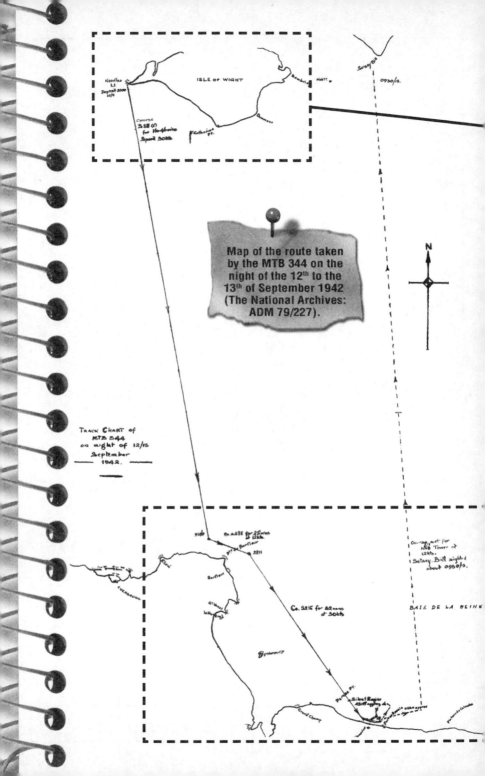

Map of the route taken by the MTB 344 on the night of the 12th to the 13th of September 1942 (The National Archives: ADM 79/227).

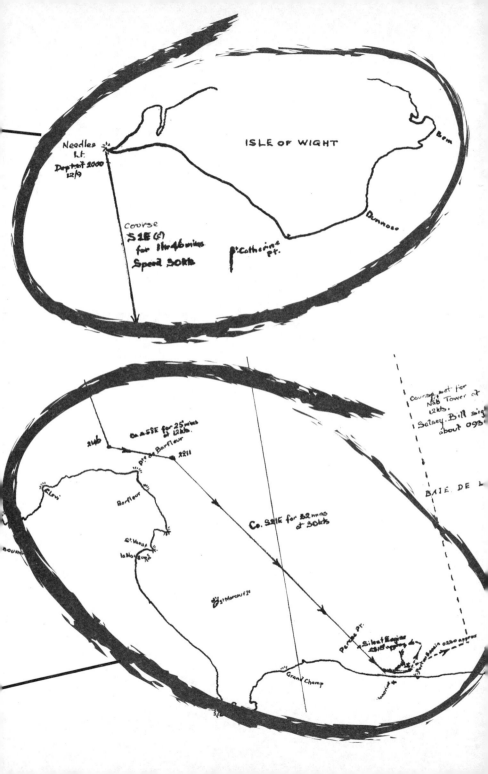

Chapter II
The defeat of operation *Aquatint*

Captain Appleyard's concentration was at its peak as the MTB 344 approached the coast. Since the vessel had passed Barfleur Point two hours previously, navigation had been a matter of informed guesswork; an uncomfortable and nerve-racking situation for all crew members. The MTB continued its course through the dense obscurity of that September night, further shrouded by occasional patches of fog. In order to avoid the minefields that the Germans had scattered throughout the Seine Bay, Lieutenant Freddie Bourne, commander of the motor boat, followed a route 4 miles from the coast towards Le Havre. And to avoid any risk of the vessel being detected from the coast, he reduced his speed to 12 knots for around 45 minutes. At that speed, the engines were relatively silent.

Bourne, at this stage of the manoeuvre, maintained his course towards the mission's target, Sainte-

Honorine-des-Pertes, of which Appleyard, as second in command, was perfectly familiar with the geographical coordinates: latitude 49° 22' N., longitude 00° 47' W. The fog finally lifted and, as the MTB progressed, the coastline became more and more visible. The commander had gradually approached the shore which was now only half a mile away. The final approach proved not only to be tricky, but dangerous. The many shallows presented a risk of grounding and the enemy was in no way to be alerted of their presence. Six miles from the target, orders were given to sound the water depth every two miles, to cut the main engine and to switch on the silent auxiliary engine. A quarter of a mile from the coast, Appleyard attentively scrutinised the 100 feet high cliffs that dominated the shores. Having meticulously scoured, with March-Phillips, the aerial photographs taken by the RAF, Appleyard had identified an indentation in the cliffside that the troop planned to climb towards a position located half a mile from the village of Sainte-Honorine. The motor boat's speed was now dead slow.

At precisely 00.05 hours[32], Appleyard noticed a small dry valley in the cliffside which he identified as the planned landmark, and immediately ordered for the engine to be cut. The commando had arrived at the shore in front of Sainte-Honorine, or at least they

---

[32] *Times are according to Captain Appleyard's report which is in GMT. One hour should be added to obtain the local time imposed by the occupant.*

West Pier
Port-en-Bessin

ENGLISH CHANNEL

Huppain

Villiers-sur-Port

D 514

Vignet-de-Cabourg

Le Grand Val

*Vertical aerial
photograph, n° 109
R 342, taken by an RAF plane
on the 26th of June 1942, to the west
of Port-en-Bessin. The arrow indicates the
precise location where Major March-Phillips'
commando should have landed, situated on the outskirts of
the village of Sainte-Honorine-des-Pertes, towards Port-en-Bessin.
(Public Record Office: DEFE 2/365)*

thought they had. However, the darkness was such that it was impossible for them to formally identify the spot where they had initially planned to ascend the cliff-side.

Nevertheless, when consulted, Major March-Phillips gave the order for the commando to land. Gus was not the sort of man who stumbled at the first hurdle. In any case, after climbing up the hill, they were sure to localise the small group of houses that they had seen on the aerial photos, and perhaps the surprise effect would even enable them to bring back a few prisoners, just like at Les Casquets Lighthouse. Once they had done so, the commando would take the same route back towards the beach, where they would re-embark with the aid of the Goatley, the famous folding boat that had been so precious to them during operation Dryad.

At 00.17 hours, the motor boat was anchored in three fathoms of water to the north west of the dry valley which led down to the sea, approximately 350 yards from the beach, not, as they thought, at Sainte-Honorine, but at Saint-Laurent-sur-Mer.

The Goatley was launched from the rear of the MTB. Eleven men climbed onboard. Major March-Phillips had Tony Hall embark first. He knew he was a machine gun ace and that if the landing turned sour, they could count on him. Then followed Captains Graham Hayes, John Burton and Francis Howard, Lieutenant André Desgrange, Sergeants Alan Williams and Tom Winter, and finally Privates Richard Lehniger, Jan Hellings and Adam Orr. The light vessel cast off from the MTB at 00.20 hours and headed straight for the dry valley. It reached the beach five minutes later. But the Major decided that the landing could not take place at this precise location which he considered to be too close to a group of houses. He therefore ordered for the Goatley to be moved farther east and the small craft was finally drawn onto the sand approximately 220 yards along the beach. The tide had been going out for two hours. The group left Captain Howard in charge of the Goatley.

For 50 minutes, the ten men explored the surrounding beach and the foot of the cliff. In total darkness, they could see no farther than five steps ahead. None of them was aware that they were in between two German "Resistance nests".

Having found nothing, they headed back for the beach and it was at that precise moment that Corporal Wichert's patrol, on its way to W.N. 29b via the path that ran along the shore, arrived on their right. It was precisely 01.05 hours, GMT (02.05 hours German time).

Suddenly, Private Kowalski's guard dog started to growl, then to bark, while pulling inland on his leash. As soon as they had heard the approaching patrol, the commandos had gone into hiding in a small hollow at the foot of the cliff amongthe shrubs. If it hadn't been for the German guard dog, they probably would never have been discovered.

Almost in unisson, Wichert and Kowalski shouted, "*Halt! Wer da?* (Halt who goes there?"). After a second warning, a gun shot was fired in their direction and Wichert retaliated with a shower of submachine gunfire. A few moments later, the British commando threw several offensive grenades towards W.N. 29b; however, they landed in the staff shelter located in the yard behind the observation post without injuring any Germans. The observation post's guards then noticed the Goatley, aground on the beach, and struck back throwing several hand grenades in the vessel's direction. Captain Appleyard, who was powerlessly observing the combat from the MTB's bridge, noted in his report, *"There were then fifteen or twenty flashes and explosions in the same vicinity which were thought to be German stick grenades, and a great deal more small arms fire".*[33]

While the rest of the patrol took refuge behind the barbed-wire fencing of the W.N. 29b post, Private Kowalski threw himself to the ground and pointed his light machine gun towards the sea. He had no time to fire a burst, before, suddenly, two of the Commando members jumped on him from behind, trying to tear his weapon from him whilst dragging him towards the

---

[33] *Public Record Office, Kew,* **Aquatint operation report** *by Captain J.G. Appleyard, Second in command of the S.S.R.F., 16ᵗʰ September 1942, Appendix (A) 2, DEFE 2/109*

ENGLISH CHANNEL

N

Landing zone

Les Moulins

Hamel-au-Prêtre

D 514

3

3A

▲
*Vertical
aerial photograph,
n° 123 R 342, taken by the
same RAF plane on the 26th of June 1942,
above the villages of Vierville-sur-Mer and
Saint-Laurent-sur-Mer. The dry valley to the right is situated
next to the locality known as "Les Moulins", to the right of which
the **Aquatint** commando landed. The dry valley to the left is situated to the west of
the locality known as "Le Hamel au Prêtre". (Public Record Office: DEFE 2/365)*

shore. The two men were Francis Howard and Tony Hall. The German struggled to such an extent that he finally freed himself and, before fleeing, managed to throw a stick grenade. Captain Howard received a splinter wound in the leg. In the scuffle, Tony Hall received a violent blow to the back of the head; a German soldier had attacked from behind with the heavy part of a stick grenade; the part containing the explosives. He lay, motionless, on the beach. Private Kowalski was then able to free himself and run back to W.N. 29b.

After the war, Tony Hall still clearly recalled this hand-to-hand combat with the German soldier, *"Hardly had we landed when we saw a German patrol coming along, and from what I remember of it... what our job was on that occasion was to get prisoners, and I remember grabbing hold of one chap, a Goon, and dragging him down to the beach and he kept saying the whole time, "Nicht Deutsch, Nicht Deutsch, Czechish, Czechish, Nicht Deutsch, Czechish", and I was sort of saying, "Oh well, we'll sort that out in the boat, you know", then somebody came up and clobbered me from behind".*[34]

[34] **Account by Tony Hall**, *from the script of the BBC radio programme broadcast on the 20th of August 1971, quoted by Mike Langley in Anders Lassen, V.C., M.C., of the S.A.S, The story of Anders Lassen and the men who fought with him, New English Library, London, 1988, page 99.*

The alarm was immediately raised by the non-commissioned officer in charge of the "Resistance nest". He immediately informed Chief Warrant Officer Pie, by telephone, that an enemy attack was underway in front of his position. The commander of "Strong point 29" then ordered the commanders of the two neighbouring W.N.s: W.N. 29a to the east on the clifftop, and W.N. 29c to the west, to launch a red star flare and a white illuminating flare, whilst maintaining fire to cover W.N. 29b.

Private Kowalski ran towards Saint-Laurent-sur-Mer, and at 01.20 hours (02.20 hours German time), he verbally alerted the Commander of the 3rd Reserve Company. He rapidly recounted his close combat with the English officers and informed of continuing conflict before "Strong point 29".

At 01.27 hours, telephone contact with the non-commissioned officer in charge of W.N. 29b confirmed the infantryman's account of events. Major Grote, consequently ordered Chief Warrant Officer Baldhusen to head towards "Strong point 29" with a non-commissioned officer and 12 men in reinforcement.

At the same time, on the beaches, the shooting had continued to rage for over half an hour, and new red, green, and often white flares coloured the seafront in a peculiar haze.

What had happened to the commando members at this precise moment of the battle?

Back on the beach, Major March-Phillips and Captain Hayes rallied their men together and ordered them to re-embark the Goatley. As well as the two officers, the following men boarded the vessel: Captain Howard who, wounded, lay at the bow, Captain Burton, Sergeants Williams and Winter, Private Lehniger, Lieutenant Desgrange and Privates Hellings and Orr. Only Lieutenant Hall, seriously wounded, was left for dead on the beach.

The Goatley managed to distance the shore some 100 yards, but the Germans very quickly detected the vessel and showered it with machine gunfire from W.N. 29c and W.N. 30a. The latter was located at Vierville-sur-Mer. The ten totally distraught men were utterly incapable of navigating the small boat out of the line of enemy fire, and, rather than making their way back to the MTB, they traced a semi-circle towards the west. The 15 ft long, 5 ft wide and 2 ft deep Goatley was soon riddled with bullets and started to take in water.

From the shore, under the light of one of the rockets, the 75 mm anti-tank gunners posted at W.N. 29c could see the Goatley's silhouette, as well as that of a larger vessel some 900 yards away. One single blast was enough to capsize the Goatley, which, nevertheless, remained above water. The gun was then aimed at the MTB. On the third fire, the motor boat was hit.

The pressure onboard was at its peak. Captain Appleyard reported the following,

"At approximately 01.20 hours, 2 machine guns on the left hand side of the gap and one on the right, all on top of the cliffs, commenced firing at her, whilst the Verey lights were directed more out to seaward. (...) A gun of some sort then opened fire on the MTB, which was now apparently clearly seen from the shore, and 6 or 8 shells passed overhead and fell further out to sea. There was no indication as to where the gun was firing from, but it presumably could not be trained down sufficiently to cover the MTB lying so close to inshore. The anchor warp was then cut and a crash start was made on the main engines at about 01.30 hours. It was then discovered that a bullet had damaged the transmission gearbox and the ignition system of the starboard engine, rendering it practically useless. A course was laid directly out to sea for two miles, and the main engines were then de-clutched and gradually throttled down for high speed to slow, to try and give the enemy the impression that the MTB was on her way home and was passing out of earshot".[35]

The situation for the members of operation Aquatint was becoming increasingly critical. All of the men onboard the Goatley had fallen overboard when the vessel had capsized. Many of them were suffering from more or less serious injuries. Major March-

---

[35] Public Record Office, Kew, **Aquatint operation report** by Captain J.G. Appleyard, Second in command of the S.S.R.F., 16th September 1942, Appendix (A) 2, DEFE 2/109.

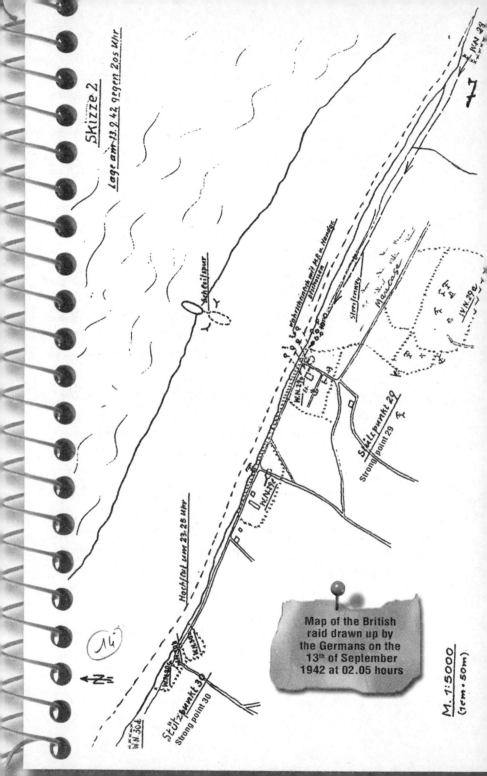

Skizze 2

Lage am 13.9.42 gegen 2os Uhr

Scheißpur

Wahrscheinlich mit Kfz u. Handgr. Schnauzen

Streifenweg

Maulwose

WN 28

(WN 29a)

WN 29b

Stützpunkt 29
Strong point 29

WN 27

Hochtal um 23.25 Uhr

(14)

N

WN 30c

WN 30b

Stützpunkt 30
Strong point 30

WN 30a

Map of the British raid drawn up by the Germans on the 13th of September 1942 at 02.05 hours

M. 1:5000
(1cm = 50m)

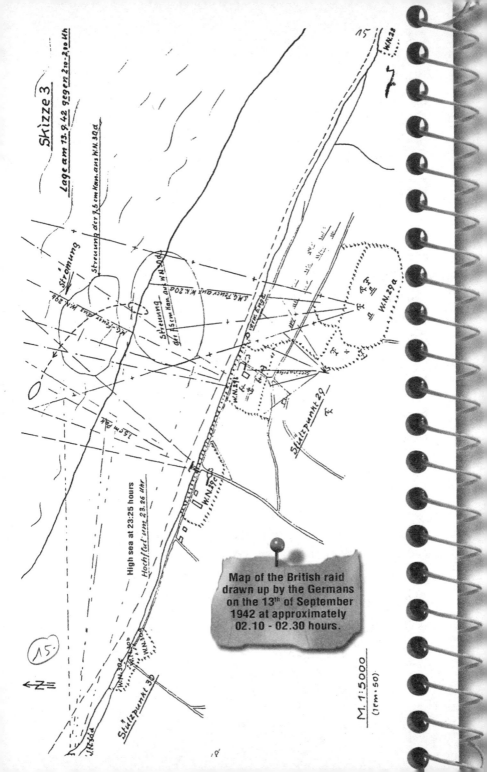

Map of the British raid drawn up by the Germans on the 13th of September 1942 at approximately 02.10 - 02.30 hours.

Phillips was, himself, severely wounded. In a vain attempt to swim back to the MTB, the Commander, utterly exhausted, finally drowned. Sergeant Williams and Private Lehniger, both suffering from shrapnel wounds, also drowned. The latter, of Czech origin, spoke excellent German. It was very probably his cries for help that Corporal Wichert's patrol had heard from the shore.

Battalion Major Grote mentioned them in his report to the 726th Infantry Regiment's high command, *"A little later, around 02.32 hours, cries for help in German were heard towards the north-west of 29c. The patrol which was making rounds between postions 29c and 30a, as well as the commander of W.N. 29c, rushed towards the cries, thinking that they had hit a German salvage vessel. They saw several men swimming towards the shore. Their boat, still close to them, could not be identified in the darkness. Two English soldiers (a captain and a non-commissioned officer) as well as a Gaullist Naval Officer were taken prisoner".*[36]

The three men, worn out, managed to laboriously reach the shore. They put up little resistance and were taken prisoner. Lord Howard of Penrith (the *"English captain"*) was literally washed up on the sand,

---

[36] *Bundesarchiv-Militärarchiv Freiburg,* **Report by Major Grote**,*13th September 1942 addressed to the Commander of the 726th Infantry Regiment, and concerning the attempted British reconnaissance mission at the 3rd Company of the 726th IR's Support base 29, page 2.*

exhausted and half-conscious. He had swallowed a great deal of sea water. His leg injury would very probably have caused him to drown had he not been lucky enough to hang onto the Goatley, still afloat. Lieutenant André Desgrange from the Free French Naval Forces (the *"Gaullist Naval Officer"*) was taken prisoner at the same time as Lord Howard. Sergeant Thomas Winter (the *"non-commissioned officer"*) was captured separately a little later, having made an attempt to swim back to the MTB.

After the war, Francis Howard resumed the dramatic emergency retreat from the beaches of Saint-Laurent-sur-Mer, *"In the scrap, I got shot in the leg and could hear the patrol saying in German, "Look, there's a boat". We got into the float, which was canvas-bottomed and not very suitable for going against the waves in a sea running a bit high. But we got a certain way out - and then everything went up. Flares and more shooting. The Goatley sank. I don't konw if it capsized or was hit by a shell. I could still swim despite my wounded leg, though not very much. Luckily, I bumped into the overturned boat which saved me. André Desgrange was on it, too. I don't know what happened to the others".*[37]

When the Goatley capsized, at least one man tried determinedly to reach the MTB which was still waiting to re-embark any men who could make their way to her; he was Sergeant Tom Winter. Uninjured, the

[37] Witness account related by Mike Langley, opus cit. page 99.

Sergeant concentrated all his efforts on reaching the motor boat, however, the darkness, the currents and the impossibility for Captain Appleyard to maintain the MTB, under enemy fire, in a constant position were all major obstacles rendering his attempts totally futile.

The motor boat's commander's behaviour was irreproachable. Let us consult Captain Appleyard's report after the hasty departure following the MTB's first anchorage, around 01.30 hours, when the vessel had just been damaged by enemy shells and gunfire,

"After about ten minutes, during which all activity ashore, except for occasional Verey lights, died down, the MTB was again headed back towards Sainte-Honorine[38] at slow speed on silent engines, showing infra-red contact light at the mast head, until within half a mile of the coast where position was maintained for the next three-quarters of an hour. During this time there was no fire on from the shore, although Verey lights still went up frequently and attempts to get the searchlight working were still continuing. None of the pre-arranged signals that the landing party were to give on returning to the MTB, or if requiring any assistance in the way of interception or picking up by the MTB, were seen, the infra-red light was burning strongly, and no trace of the landing craft was seen at sea, although what had previously been thought

---

[38] *The village was, in fact, Saint-Laurent-sur-Mer. When drafting his report, Captain Appleyard was still unaware of the Commando's error **concerning its landing point.***

to be the landing craft lying on the beach could still be seen in the light of the flares".

Just as the German patrols were capturing the three members of the commando, and as they discovered Tony Hall's body, motionless on the beach, Chief Warrant Officer Pie from the 3rd Company of the 726th IR telephoned, at 02.15 hours, to Second Lieutenant Bierhoff, commander of W.N. 25c at Port-en-Bessin. "Strong point 29's" observation posts had just detected another enemy vessel a few hundred yards from the landing point. This vessel was, of course, the MTB 344.

Appleyard pursued,

"At 02.25 hours, 7 or 8 shells were fired from N.W. of the MTB all passing overhead and pitching between her and the shore. These were apparently fired at close range by a patrol craft, possibly 2 or 3-pounder ammunition. Immediately afterwards upward of a dozen shells were fired from a different ship to the N. of the MTB, the nearest of which fell twenty feet on the starboard beam deluging the boat with water. The MTB had apparently been spotted from seaward against the light of the flares on shore, and further Verey lights again went up, and the MG's ashore on the cliffs again opened a very inaccurate fire".[39]

Ten minutes later, Captain Appleyard, with death in his soul, resigned himself to casting off and gave the order to do so. Any further lingering would jeopardise the

---

[39] *Public Record Office, Kew,* **Aquatint operation report** *by Captain J.G. Appleyard, Second in command of the S.S.R.F., 16th September 1942, Appendix (A) 3, DEFE 2/109.*

MTB's crew members. The German patrols had, by now, very probably left Grandcamp and Port-en-Bessin, and were capable of encircling the motor boat in no time.

"Course was immediately set to the Eastward for about one mile and then to the Northward direct for the NAB tower. A departure was taken at 02.35 hours. Nothing further was seen of the patrol craft to seaward, and the return passage was made at a speed of about 12 knots in a rising sea and swell, wind force 4.

In view of the greatly reduced speed of the MTB it was considered less of a risk to pass directly through the enemy minefield than to attempt the much longer return passage via Cape Barfleur around the end of the minefield, and along the main inshore shipping route. The minefield was crossed without incident.

Air cover located the MTB at 06.45 hours, but left again after twenty minutes owing to bad flying conditions. The MTB docked at Portsmouth at 10.35 hours".[40]

One can imagine Captain Appleyard's state of mind. He had just lost his comrades and best friends, Gus and Graham. Were they dead? Were they wounded? Had they been taken prisoner? What would he tell their families? How would the SOE chiefs and Combined Operations react to such a disaster? The young British officer, second in command of the SSRF, was enduring the most agonising hours of his existence since the beginning of the war.

[40] *Idem, Appendix (A) 3.*

Chapter III
A disastrous outcome

From a military point of view

The day after his return from mission, Geoffrey Appleyard took the first train for London. He was to give an oral account of events to the SOE chiefs in Baker Street. He then spent half a day, on the 16th of September, drafting his written operation report. Several copies of his report were then made and they were dispatched respectively to the SOE's military chief, General Colin Gubbins, to Combined Operations headquarters, to the Admiralty, etc.

Appendix "B" of the Aquatint operation report was signed by I.C. Collins, "G.S.O.2." (General Staff Officer Grade 2). He gave his assessment of the operation and listed, in twelve points, the lessons that were to be learned and the remarks that were to be taken into consideration. This document is worth analysing, and should be compared with our current knowledge of events during operation Aquatint.

"1. The risk of carrying out a frontal assault even on a supposedly lightly defended objective is considerable. The plan was to land on a very small beach further east and climb up a narrow gully but this opening could not be found on a very dark night, and plans had to be changed".

This point implicitly repudiates the initial operation plan as proposed by Combined Operations. The German defence had clearly been underestimated. Such defence would have been lesser at Sainte-Honorine-des-Pertes, the high cliffs at this location being far less vulnerable than the dry valleys which offered potential access to the shore. Furthermore, it appears evident that the target had not been clearly identified during the operation's preparatory phase. The mistaken landing point, clearly demonstrates that the information provided by the Admiralty's naval maps, the military intelligence maps and the Michelin guide…, all cross-checked with aerial photographs, was insufficient.

"2. The assault craft must be landed on a beach where a safe and quick get away can be effected".

A vast beach such as that of Saint-Laurent-sur-Mer/Vierville, situated in the firing line of several machine guns and 75 mm cannons, retrospectively appears to be a very badly chosen spot for a commando operation.

"3. An extra boat was carried in M.T.B. but under the circumstances could not be used: where possible, forces should go ashore in two boats".

The MTB was equipped with a "Doris" lifeboat which was far more resistant than the Goatley, but was not used during the operation. Following operation Dryad, during which the Goatley had successfully transported the entire commando plus seven prisoners, March-Phillips and his men had somewhat overestimated the vessel's technical prowess; hence the decision to use the Goatley, and only the Goatley. The simultaneous use of the Doris during the landing operation may have enabled some of the men to return to the MTB.

"4. M.T.B. incurred too great a risk in lying so close off-shore and was lucky not to be sunk".

This remark appears to be perfectly justified. The MTB 344 had approached the shore to enable the commandos to re-embark as quickly as possible. In doing so, the vessel exposed itself to enemy fire from the German "Resistance nests" to such an extent that a 75 mm shell landed close to the wheelhouse and machine gunfire hit the starboard engine. However, the damage was purely material and the motor boat's crew members had been particularly fortunate, all the more so since an electrical failure had prevented the Germans from using one of their powerful search lights.

"5. A plan should be made in advance where a pick up can be effected 2 - 3 nights later in case some of party get left behind".

Instantaneously, this remark appears rather surprising. How was it possible to know whether the men left behind were dead, prisoners, or, on the contrary, out of the enemy clutches? However, as we will learn later, such a precautionary measure may have saved Captain Hayes.

"6. M.T.B. may have been picked up off Barfleur when she passed within 5 miles to avoid minefield, but there is no proof of this, though it is noticeable how quickly the whole stretch of coast was alert immediately the alarm was given".

The German reports prove that the British motor boat had not been detected as it hugged the Barfleur coast towards Saint-Laurent-sur-Mer. The vessel's relatively small size (60 ft long), its high speed and its streamlined shape rendered it very difficult to detect on German radar systems, hence its use in such operations. Furthermore, the thick clouds on that night of the 12th of September had reduced visibility to a maximum of 40 feet, preventing the "Strong point's" different observation posts from making any visual contact. And finally, the heavy blankets of fog mentioned in Appleyard's report are not to be neglected.

The German communications system did, in fact, react relatively quickly, as indicated in the 716th IR Commander, General Matterstock's assessment report (Erfahrungen). The entire landing sector was placed under level 2 alarm at precisely 02.32 hours (German time), exactly 27 minutes after the first contact between the commando and Corporal Wichert's patrol at 02.05 hours. The entire 726th IR was on level 2 alert at 02.35 hours, as well as the whole sector situated to the west around Vierville, where the 3rd Battalion was stationed.

Throughout the day of the 13th of September, the entire command chain was alerted, from Colonel Münstermann of the 726th Infantry Regiment to the Commander of the 7th Army himself, General Friedrich Dollmann, in Le Mans.

"7. M.T.B. on return journey crossed minefield with no mishaps".

Appleyard had obliged Lieutenant Bourne to take a great risk in sailing the MTB 344 across the Seine Bay minefield; a risk further exacerbated by the deteriorating weather conditions. While the wind was estimated to be force 2 at midnight (as stated in the final German report), it had risen to force 4 around 02.30 hours (Appleyard's report), thus rendering the already damaged motor boat more difficult to manoeuvre. But did they really have the choice but to cross that mine-field, with one of the engines damaged and practically out of use? The officer who wrote the above note, made no value judgement on the subject. The motor boat's crew had, on that night, been very lucky.

"8. The navigation throughout seems to have been excellent".

This remark is a genuine compliment to Captain Appleyard, and to Lieutenant Freddie Bourne.

However, it in no way masks the navigation error made on the outward journey, and leading the commando to land at Saint-Laurent-sur-Mer instead of Sainte-Honorine-des-Pertes.

"9. It is strongly recommended that as soon as possible another raid is carried out for sake of morale; next suggested raid (Island of Sark) to be carried out approximately 20 Sept. The fact must be faced that we are certain to have some mishaps".

Here again, the stakes were high. The remaining members of the SSRF, with added reinforcements from N°12 Commando as suggested by Collins in point 10 of his report, did indeed carry out another raid on the Island of Sark in the Channel Islands, on the night of the 3rd of October 1942. The operation, led by Captain Appleyard, was given the codename: Basalt. However, this new mission also met with misfortune and even had regrettable consequences on the detention conditions for the 1,700 Canadians taken prisoner during the Dieppe raid on the 19th of August 1942.[41]

"10. Every encouragement should be given to S.S.R.F. to bring their numbers back to normal. Capt. Appleyard is seeing Brig. Gubbins. A detachment from N°12 Commando could probably be made available immediately".

With the loss of eleven men during operation Aquatint, the SSRF had indeed lost a fifth of its total number of recruits, MTB crew members included, and a third of its commandos.[42]

Less than a month after Aquatint, Major General Colin Gubbins, chief of the SOE had five men transferred from the N°12 Commando to the SSRF to take part in operation Basalt.

"11. Captain Appleyard, M.C. to be appointed S.S.R.C."

It appeared logical that Captain Appleyard, already awarded with the Military Cross and who had been second in command of the SSRF during Aquatint, be put forward to become its commander. Three weeks later, it was done, and he commanded operation Basalt on the Island of Sark.

"12. Question of awards to S.S.R.F."

Major March-Phillips was awarded a posthumous MBE - Member of the British Empire.

---

[41] *The SOE's official historian, M.R.D. Foot, resumes in this manner operation **Basalt** and its consequences in his book: S.O.E. in France, London, Her Majesty's Stationery Office, London, 1966, page 186: "SSRF never recovered from his death (March-Phillips) and from the aftermath of the **Sark raid** - five prisoners had been taken; four had tried to escape, and were dispatched at once; and one of them was found next day stabbed to the heart with his hands tied behind his back. Several thousand Canadians captured at Dieppe were manacled for some months in reprisal". Following operation **Basalt**, Hitler ordered for all captured commandos, armed or not, in uniform or in civilian dress, to be executed without exception.*

[42] *According to Sir Brooks Richards, The Secret Flotillas, Clandestine Sea Operations in the Mediterranean, North Africa and the Adriatic 1940-44 M.D.V., 2001, page 226, "From 9 at the creation of the **Maid Honor Force**, the SSRF staff finally comprised 55 officers and men".*

The severe defeat of operation Aquatint had probably already sealed the fate of the SSRF. The deplorable consequences of operation Basalt on the Island of Sark were only to accelerate Combined Operations' decision to put an end to the Small Scale Raiding Force. The force was finally disbanded in April 1943 after operation Huckaback on the night of the 27th of February 1943 on Herm and Jethou, two of the channel Islands.

THE HUMAN LOSSES

What had become of the eleven men from operation Aquatint?

At around 05.00 hours (German time), at low tide, the Germans discovered the bodies of three English soldiers. At dawn, they were able to identify their rank and their military badges: a Commander (Major), a Sergeant and a Private. They simultaneously discovered a capsized landing craft riddled with bullet holes, the Goatley.[43] Inside the vessel, they found a 2

---

[43] *The German Division report signed by General Matterstock, gives a detailed description:* **"Lifeboat. Examination of the lifeboat gave the following indications: 4.65 metres long, 1.60 metres wide (from exterior edge to exterior edge). Planking height approximately 60 cm. It is a lifeboat of extremely lightweight construction, with a perfectly flat keel. It can be dismantled and folded, and subsequently transported within an extremely small space. The planking is comprised of a frame with a taut sail canvas. The keel comprises a single plank of wood: good landing possibilities on a sandy beach. Tests have demonstrated that the lifeboat is capable, at a push, of transporting up to 13 men closely seated".**

gallon demijohn of drinking water. With no precise knowledge of the number of men having taken part in the raid, they estimated that at least 10 had attempted to land. The four prisoners, together with the three bodies, gave a total of already seven men. Three waist belts washed up by the incoming tide and belonging to neither the prisoners nor the dead enabled the Germans to confirm this estimation which was very close to reality.

A few hours later, the four prisoners were taken to the Standortkommandantur in Vierville. Tony Hall, who was very seriously wounded, was immediately transported to the military hospital in Caen. Lord Howard and André Desgrange, captured together, were soon joined by Tom Winter who had been captured later, and they were all three detained in a double-locked room. Captain Howard, who suffered from leg injuries, was lying on the floor. Suddenly, a German officer entered into the room and ordered them to empty the contents of their pockets onto the table. He then, in plain language, announced that they were to be executed because they were commandos. Before their execution, they were to wait there for a military intelligence officer who was on his way from Caen to question them.

During the initial interrogation, the German Abwehr officer, Commander Köster, obtained little information. Captain Howard refused to answer his questions. Winter and Desgrange complied only to giving very vague indications, which were recorded in the secret report addressed to the commander of the 716th Infantry Division.

"The boat left England to cross the Channel on the 12th of September towards a destination that was yet unknown to the troops. Later, they boarded a smaller vessel and sailed towards the shore. The crew of this smaller vessel comprised 11 men. They refused to give the total number of men on the larger vessel. There was a second boat attached to the large vessel, which was due to follow as soon as the first small vessel arrived at shore (a light signal was planned). Faced with the question concerning the commandos' mission, Winter and Desgrange replied: capture of prisoners and gathering information".[44]

The following morning, on the 14th of September, the Germans came to collect Tom Winter and André Desgrange, the only two of the raid's commandos totally unscathed, to take them to the beach at Saint-Laurent. Once on the beach, they desolately discovered the death of three of their comrades. Their remains still lay, lined up on the beach 150 yards or so from the pathway. They were then ordered to carry the bodies of Major March-Phillips, Sergeant Williams and Private Lehniger past the watermark, in other words above the beach. When they noticed a German officer

---

[44] *Bundesarchiv, Militärarchiv, Freiburg,* **Secret report of 13th September 1942** *addressed by the IG Commander to the Staff of the 716th Infantry Division.*

filming the scene, they immediately realised that the Nazi propaganda would lay its hands on the event and take full advantage of it. Both prisoners were then taken to Bayeux, to the 726th IR headquarters.

On Tuesday 15th September, at 09.00 hours, and in the greatest solemnity, the Germans had the three British soldiers buried in the cemetery at Saint-Laurent-sur-Mer. Two inhabitants of Saint-Laurent, M Jules Scelles and a WWI veteran, M Henri Leroutier, watched the scene from behind a wall at the Hôtel du Carrefour [45]. No inhabitants had been allowed to take part in the ceremony. The three coffins, covered with flowers and transported by three carts were preceded by a section of the 3rd Reserve Company stationed at Saint-Laurent, and followed by German officers. The coffins were then lowered into the three graves that had been dug side by side. Then, to close the ceremony, a guard of honour fired a three gun salute. The entire scene was filmed and the Germans gave a succinct account of the event to the Calvados Prefect [46]. The German Propaganda services had decided to make maximum profit of the event. The idea was to exhibit the rectitude with which the Wehrmacht paid tribute to the dead, even those from the enemy, whilst the latter, via its commandos, did not hesitate to use the most cowardly and dishonourable methods.

[45] *Operation **Aquatint**, a British commando lands at Saint-Laurent-sur-Mer on the night of the 12th of September 1942, **39/45 Magazine**, n° 65, Heimdal, Bayeux, 1991, pages 13-21.*

[46] *Calvados Departmental Archives, **Reports by the Calvados Prefect from 1939 to 1944**. Soon to be published.*

On their return to detention, Tom Winter and André Desgrange discovered that, during the night, their companion Francis Howard had been transferred to the Clémenceau hospital in Caen. In the afternoon, the two men were then separated and Tom Winter was never again to see his French comrade.

The British Sergeant was driven by lorry to the 716th Infantry Division's headquarters in Caen, escorted by a guard and an officer from military intelligence.

The second interrogation took place at the division's command post, situated in the Avenue de Bagatelle. The Germans used several techniques to make Winter talk: from psychological pressure and intimidation to bodily violence. On the first day, the Division's commander, General Matterstock himself, came to question the Sergeant at length. The following day, Winter was forced to abandon his uniform and to change into German civilian dress. After a meticulous search, his uniform finally revealed a few secrets: the epaulettes contained a hidden map that was destined to be used should he manage to escape. There is even an anecdote: under Winter's Sergeant Major badge, the Germans were somewhat surprised to find a small piece of tartan fabric.

Tom Winter was later to recount, *"An SS officer asked me what the padding was. I said, "Scotch plaid" - and got a wallop for it. They found the maps hidden in my epaulettes but missed my secret fly buttons. One held above the other formed a compass"*.[47]

For eight long days and nights, Tom Winter was submitted to prolonged, exhausting and often brutal interrogation. *"I had, however, a very good cover story, as I had belonged to the R.A.S.C. (Royal Army Service Corps), and said I knew nothing as I only carried stores for the others. The Germans could not find anything to the contrary as my regimental number confirmed this"*.[48]

The Germans finally obtained very little further information to supplement their own conclusions, which were summarised in the second part of their secret report.

"They belonged to the crew of a special small motor boat which left Portsmouth on the 12th of September at around 21.00 hours. The vessel was of a new type, specially built for commando landings.

Construction of the vessel: this vessel measures 85 feet long and 10 feet wide. It is built of wood and has a combustion engine. Speed 56 knots with a sloping stern. The rear construction is designed so that a smaller vessel can be lowered into the sea via a roller system.

There were two embarkations onboard (one rather large vessel equipped with oars, and another smaller lifeboat).

The entire crew comprised 17 men.

---

[47] *Mike Langley, opus cit. page 101.*

[48] *Public Record Office, Kew, DEFE 2/365, "**Account by S.M. Winter** on operation "**Aquatint**" which took place against Sainte-Honorine-des-pertes on night 12/13 September 1942". undated, page 2.*

After manoeuvres in the Channel, the boat arrived at the landing point at approximately 01.00 hours. Immediately afterwards, the rowing boat was launched with 11 men onboard, at approximately a mile and a half off the coast. The tide was already going out (high sea on the 13-9 at 00.46 hours). The crew was already experiencing difficulties with the sea conditions and considered their attempts to be hazardous. At 01.30 hours, the small boat landed and was abandoned by its crew. While the majority of the crew remained 30 yards or so from the sea, their commander, Major March-Phillips, together with Captain Lord Howard, set out on a reconnaissance mission of strong point 29. On their attempted return to the landing point at approximately 02.30 hours, they met with a patrol (with a guard dog) which opened fire on them. After having thrown a few hand grenades against resistance nest 29b, the crew fled towards their boats whilst one of them endeavoured to drag along a prisoner. One of the crew members did not make it to the boat (Lieutenant T.A.T. Hall). As soon as the crew boarded the boat, it was rapidly attacked by light and heavy machine gunfire, and later by a shell. The vessel was immediately hit, at a distance of approximately 400 yards from the beach, and capsized. The crew cried for help and it is supposed that a lifeboat was sent from the larger vessel. Captain Lord Howard, Lieutenant Desgrange and Sergeant Winter swam to the shore. The other occupants most probably *drowned. The prisoners confirmed that the grounded vessel next to resistance nest 29c was in fact the vessel that had been launched from the speed boat at approximately 01.00 hours. Concerning the embarkation, it was indeed a wooden boat with a sail. This wooden boat was 40 feet long, 9 to 10 feet wide and 3 feet deep. Research revealed that the vessel comprised a crew of 14 men.*[49]

The declarations lead us to believe that this operation was carried out by a special commando trained for landing missions. The acquired practical experience was later to be used in instruction. Indeed, the commando comprised soldiers from different battalions.

Only Major March-Phillips knew the mission's precise objective. Lieutenant Desgrange claimed that he had learned, from conversation, that the mission concerned Port-en-Bessin".[50]

The Germans also used cunning to try to obtain further information on the raid, by sending Tom Winter to the Clémenceau hospital in Caen, thus enabling him to talk to Captain Howard and Lieutenant Hall who had both been admitted to the same hospital room. Tony Hall was still unconscious during his visit, but

---

[49] *This figure is false. The commando comprised* **eleven men.**

[50] *Bundesarchiv, Militärarchiv, Freiburg,* **Secret report of 13th September 1942** *addressed by the IG Commander to the Staff of the 716th Infantry Division, pages 1-2-3*

Lord Howard was already on the road to recovery. Howard managed to hint to Winter that their conversation was very probably being recorded, and both men therefore indulged in a cryptic discussion until the end of the visit.

Two days later, Tom Winter was transferred by train, to Rennes, while Captain Howard and Lieutenant Hall remained in Caen. His precise place of detention is unknown to us, but three days after his arrival, Tom Winter discovered that Captain Burton, Private Orr and Private Hellings were detained in the same location. The Germans had John Burton and Tom Winter placed in the same cell, whilst Jan Hellings and Adam Orr were placed, together, in a cell directly opposite. Delighted to be finally reunited, the prisoners were at last able to communicate with each other and to exchange their respective versions of the turn of events since their unfortunate landing on the beach at Saint-Laurent-sur-Mer.

Unfortunately, we have no witness accounts from the three fugitives that were captured on the 17th of September. Only Tom Winter recounts, in a few lines, what had become of the three men before being captured a few days after Lord Howard.

"Apparently they had all swum down and met below the verey lights further west. They had then travelled down country, but had encountered unfortunately, a German parachute company which happened to be undergoing exercises in the area".[51]

The five men were detained a further eight to ten days in Rennes before being sent to POW camps. During their transfer, the men were split into two groups: the officers were sent to an Oflag, the non-commissioned officers and the men from the ranks were sent to a Stalag. Hence, Winter, Hellings and Orr found themselves travelling to Frankfurt in the same train. At their arrival, Winter was distressed at seeing his two colleagues separated from him and taken away by the Gestapo. The German police were intrigued by their nationalities and wanted to know how a Dutchman and a Pole had managed to leave their homeland to enlist in the British Army.

Consequently, Tom Winter arrived alone at Stalag VIII B, a POW camp situated in Lamsdorf (today known as Lambinowice) in Poland.

Captain Burton and Lieutenant Desgrange also took the road to exile and captivity towards a POW camp for officers.

---

[51] *Public Record Office, Kew, "**Account by S.M. Winter** on operation **"Aquatint"** which took place against Sainte-Honorine-des-Pertes on night 12/13 September 1942", DEFE 2/365, 2 pages.*

CHAPTER IV
HOW GERMAN PROPAGANDA EXPLOITED THE EVENT

The British raid provoked two types of reaction in France: a German military reaction which, after having caused the mission's defeat, rapidly took advantage of it in propaganda terms, and a reaction from the French administrative authorities who could but record an event that was far beyond their understanding.

THE DEFEAT OF AQUATINT CONTRIBUTED TO GERMAN PROPAGANDA

On the German side, operation Aquatint generated an abundant harvest of reports of all sorts and at all levels of the military chain of command.

In chronological order, the first report was drafted on the 13ᵗʰ of September 1942, only a few hours after the British landing attempt. The report was for the attention of the commander of the 726th Infantry Division, Colonel (Oberst) Münstermann, whose headquarters were in Bayeux. It comprised three typewritten pages, signed by the Battalion Major Grote. In view of the preliminary conclusions at dawn of the 13th of September, and of the first prisoner interrogations, the Germans had already collected a great deal of information: the men from the commando had arrived close to the coast aboard a rather large boat which they disembarked to board a smaller vessel, a long embarkation (which had been found on the sand at low tide) before landing on the beach. They also knew that the commando comprised eleven men, four of whom had since disappeared. The military rank of the dead and of the prisoners was now known based on their military badges and on information obtained during interrogation. They had also identified, among the three survivors, a French officer from the Free French Naval Forces, who had immediately been classified as a "Gaullist".

A second report rated "Secret" and dated 13th September, but very probably antedated, was sent by Colonel Münstermann to the commander of the 716th Infantry Division, General Matterstock. The report was based on information obtained during interrogation of the only two valid prisoners (André Desgrange and Tom Winter), the first having taken place at the 726th IR combat post in Bayeux, and the second at the Division's Command Post in Caen. These interrogations had enabled the Germans to ascertain that the commando had left Portsmouth on the 12th of September at approximately 21.00 hours, aboard a small speed boat of an innovative concept specially designed for landing missions. They also now knew the rank, the identity, the age and the affiliation of the three soldiers found dead on the beach: *"Major March-Phillips, 34 years, infantry"*, whose identification badge had been found, *"Sergeant Williams, 21 years, infantry"*, and *"Private Richard Leonard, 39 years, infantry"*, for whom the report even mentioned his regimental number: 6387011.[52]

At the third level of military hierarchy, General Matterstock then sent a report, also rated "Secret" and antedated the 13th of September 1942, to General Behlendorff, Commander of the LXXXIV Army Corps in Saint-Lô. This report, which included the two previous reports from the inferior military ranks, contained several detailed diagrams of the conditions of the British landing attempt and of the German military reaction. The commander general of the 716th IR gave a detailed assessment of the operation and drew a certain number of conclusions and lessons to be learned concerning the organisation of German coastal

---

[52] *This **regimental number**, noted by the Germans, does not coincide with the regimental number inscribed on Richard Lehniger-Leonard's grave in the cemetery in Saint-Laurent-sur-Mer (13801849). It does however coincide, to within one figure (6387010), with the regimental number indicated for Abraham Opoczynski by the Commonwealth War Commission.*

defence (weapons, communication, tactical measures). The importance of guard dogs was emphasised in his report, *"Guard dogs and patrol dogs are the best of sentries. The very least of the dog's reactions should be scrutinised and conclusions should be drawn. There should be a guard dog in every Resistance Nest, to scent human presence and to raise the alert. Dogs should therefore be acquired and placed where there are currently none. Do not spoil the dogs but train them to be vigilant"*.

We do not have in our possession reports from the superior military ranks, including the report drafted by General Behlendorff, commander of the LXXXIV Army Corps and addressed to the commander general of the 7th Army, Friedrich Dollmann whose headquarters were situated in Le Mans, and the report from the latter to the Führer's high command headquarters in Berlin.

The High Command in Berlin was fast to react to operation Aquatint by using the raid's defeat to feed Nazi propaganda. The first press release on the subject was transmitted by the official German press agency as early as the 14th of September 1942, at 12.50 hours. This release was immediately published, over the following days, by many German and occupied territory newspapers. In France, the press release appeared in the headlines of many regional and national dailies: **Paris-Soir** (15/09/42), **Ouest-Eclair** (15/09/42), **le Journal de Normandie** (15/09/42), **la Presse Caennaise** (16/09/42), etc...

The press release was published as follows, with a few translation variations depending on the newspapers involved, *"On the night of the 12th to the 13th of September, a British landing corps comprising 5 officers, a warrant officer and a soldier, attempted to set foot on the French Channel coast to the East of Cherbourg.*

Detected at their first approach action, the defence opened fire on them: the landing craft was sunk by a shell, several of the assailants were taken prisoner, of whom three English officers and a Gaullist Naval officer.

The bodies of a commander, a warrant officer and a solider were found".[53]

On the following day, the 15th of September, a second press release was broadcast by the German High Command, at 00.49 hours, as follows,

"Berlin: The following details of the failed reconnaissance attempt led by the British on the Cotentin coast have been forwarded by the German High Command on Monday evening. In the early hours of the morning of the 13th of September, the German coast guards located an embarkation close to the coast. Several men jumped overboard to run to the shore. The boat then attempted to turn and head for the high seas, abandoning several of its crew members. However, the

---

[53] *Report reproduced in the* **Ouest-Eclair**, *Tuesday 15th September 1942, entitled:* **Hit and run attack repelled close to Cherbourg.**

boat was severely hit by a shell and sank. Those who had landed were taken prisoner after a short period of gunfire.

The prisoners, as the survivors of the wreck, were all British officers, except one man: a Gaullist Naval officer. Several British officers were killed including a commander. The German troops took possession of a wooden embarkation, a raft and three machine guns".

The Normandy press, just like the Parisian press,[54] strictly censored by the German Propaganda Staffel, broadcast the press release received from the Führer's High Command headquarters on the 14th of September at 12.50 hours,

"On the night of the 12th to the 13th of September, a British landing corps comprising 5 officers, a warrant officer and a soldier, attempted to set foot on the French Channel coast to the East of Cherbourg. The unit's approach was immediately detected by German defence which opened fire. The landing craft was sunk by a shell.

We took prisoner three English officers and a Gaullist Naval officer. We found the bodies of a commander, a warrant officer and a soldier".

---

[54] *The daily* **Paris-Soir**, *in its last issue, dated Tuesday 15th September 1942, published the press release in its headline entitled:* **Six Englishmen and a Gaullist attempt to land near Cherbourg. They are killed or taken prisoner.**

In Caen, **the Journal de Normandie**, dated Tuesday 15th September 1942, covered the title in a framed article with the headline, *"An English hit and run attack fails to the East of Cherbourg. Four officers taken prisoner"*. In its Wednesday 16th of September issue, **the Presse Caennaise**, a daily evening newspaper, published the release verbatim among a list of all of the releases received from the Führer's high command headquarters on the 14th.

The Bessin press published the first German press release somewhat after the event: **The Courrier du Bessin**, a daily newspaper covering the towns of Bayeux, Balleroy, Isigny, Trévières, Caumont, Ryes and Saint-Clair, in its 17th to 24th September issue and **the Journal de Bayeux** in the headline of its Friday 18th September 1942 issue.

Strangely enough, the second press release which was more detailed than the first, and that we traced in the British archives, does not appear to have been published in the press.

On the other hand, a rather long article entitled *"The Cherbourg night"*[55], was published in a German magazine.[56]

---

[55] *This is also the title of the **propaganda film** based on the event.*

[56] *We have, unfortunately, been unable to find the name of this **magazine**.*

"13 September 1942
The Cherbourg night

This time it was an "Officercommando" collecting "Experience".
Black is the night. Tides whisper. Infantrymen of the coastal guard stand at their posts, the strip connecting two strong points. They start on a fresh circuit. Hardly have they left the wire defences of the strong point before the watchdog barks. What can it be? Calmly, the soldiers stand and stare into the darkness. A shadow, darker than the night, slowly takes shape. Can it be a boat? One of them lifts a stone and throws it in the direction of this indefinite shape. A cry, shots crackle - Enemy! Enemy! The machine gunner throws himself flat and brings his gun into position, too late, two - three of them heave him up and drag him to the boat which has been left on the beach at high water mark. The resistance of the soldier becomes weaker and he lets himself slump. But he has already taken a hand-grenade from his belt, now, a pull at the fuse string, and with the strength of desperation wrenches himself free. The grenade splinters between the enemy, all in a few fleeting seconds, three, four explosions, over there beside the "Spanish Horsemen"[57], the light of the grenades licks up viciously.

---

[57] *The Germans referred to the "chevaux-de-frise", defence systems involving a central wooden bar with crossed spikes, as "spanische reiter" - in English "**Spanish horsemen**".*

Alarm, alarm, hand grenades hail into the strong-point. Between the fantastic licking flames the infantry-men run to their alarm positions.

Alarm, alarm, it is not a minute since the incident began, already the defences have opened up. A machine gun starts to hammer, a second, a third joins in, now already, crossfire commences from a neigh-bouring strong point. Between rocket flares, the coloured signal goes up. Behind, shells howl startlingly, in a barrage.

Now, the gun is firing, which stands right down on the beach. In the light of the flare rockets, the gun commander has made out a boat, which is lying some 400 metres out to sea. The first shell falls short, the second improves. Fire! The third - direct hit. The ship sinks.

Just as surprisingly as the alarm flares up, so it dies. The enemy moves no more. Already, the guards leave the strong point and comb the beach. Then come the few who can save themselves by swimming into captivity. Winded, exhausted, and completely finished, they stagger up with raised hands. Slowly the day breaks, the tide recedes, and leaves some of the victims free. Here is a young English major, drowned. Here is one of his British Majesty's sergeants, who lies with bloated face and smashed eyes, in his own blood. Equipment, weapons, a rubber boat, another corpse - that is the dismal end of the undertaking. And inside, in the quarters of the commander, prisoners, pale as death, with tired flickering gazes, all officers. They did *their hard duty, and came to gain experience. Now they have their experience - losses, evidence of failure. War correspondent, Ralph Urbanetz".*[58]

This text was sent to us by Tom winter who explained, in a letter addressed to André Heintz on the 23rd of January 1986, reproduced below, how he found this document. In accordance with German propaganda strategy and with a dose of poetic licence, the author of the article tried to demonstrate to his readers that the British landing attempts were, and always would be, futile, as the ironic conclusion very clearly suggests. The account of the raid, as experienced by the Germans, is globally accurate, if one accepts the author's deliberate mistake in stating that all of the commandos were officers.

Here is what Tom Winter wrote to André Heintz:

"23rd January 1986

Dear André,
Thank you very much for your Christmas card (…).
I am enclosing a copy of the German version of our raid at St-Laurent/Ste-Honorine. It was not quite like their report.

---

[58] **Translation of the article from German to English, given to André Heintz** by Tom Winter.

When I got back to the beach, after a long swim, German soldiers took me to an army post where I met André Desgrange. He told me that Lieutenant Hall was wounded and taken to hospital and that Lord Howard was wounded and was in the next room.

When daylight came, André and I were taken down to the beach. It was low tide and we could see three bodies. Our guards made us drag them up the beach above the high tide mark. Then our guards took us to Bayeux. There, we were separated. That was the last I saw of André Desgrange.

I have accounted for seven of our party. There were four more who swam west along the coast. One of them was Graham Hayes. You know what he went through and his tragic end in Fresnes prison in Paris. I did meet up with the other three.

My interrogation started. The following day I was taken to Caen where it continued for three or four days. It was on the last day of my interrogation in Caen, while waiting for my interrogating officer, that I saw the report of our raid in a German newspaper lying on the table. A few minutes later a soldier came into the room and spoke to my guard for a few minutes. That gave me enough time to tear the report out of the newspaper and into my pocket.

My next move was by train from Caen to Rennes, Bretagne. Two days after my arrival in Rennes, the last three men of our party were brought in. They were taken prisoner by a German patrol, not very far from Rennes.

They were Captain John Burton, Jan Hellings, a Dutchman and Adam Orr, a Polish Jew. His name, Adam Orr was a nom de guerre. John Burton was put in my cell and Hellings and Orr shared a cell next door. I was with them for two days. Then I was taken away by a two-guard escort on a long train journey to Poland, stopping at German military barracks en route to rest and eat. I was taken to Stalag 8B, shackled, and put in a compound with other commandos having the same treatment. Some months later I did meet up with Hellings, and in the same camp.

So, André, this is my account of the raid at St-Laurent/Ste-Honorine as I saw it (...)".

The unsuccessful British raid on Saint-Laurent was a godsend for the Propaganda Staffel which had an antenna in Caen in one of the offices of the Feldkommandantur 723. Orders were given for a film to be shot onsite by a war correspondent from the Propaganda Company: SS Sonderführer Urbanetz, the same correspondent who had written Tom Winter's souvenir article, together with a photographer, Corporal Schönemann. The Germans possessed the bodies of three British soldiers, Major March-Phillips, Sergeant Williams and Private Leonard, but also equipment left on the beach: the 40 ft long landing craft inside which they found a sail, 5 submachine guns, a few grenades, and the military gear washed up by the sea until the 13th of September at 22.00 hours: 12

paddles, 3 waist belts equipped with pistol and dagger, a bag with two grenades and a naval anchor with the following inscription: *"Made in England. J. + W.S. Patent. COR. 45"* to which a 40 ft hemp rope from the larger vessel, the MTB 344, was attached. It was more than they needed to prove the material facts.

They now needed to present them in such a manner as to demonstrate the efficiency of the German coastal defence and the consequent tragic futility of any British landing attempts. It was also crucial for them to display the German army's rectitude in dealing with the dead, all be they adversaries. Hence the organisation of an official funeral ceremony with coffins, wagons, sheaves of flowers, procession by a section of infantrymen from the Wehrmacht, together with their officers, and a military salute fired from the town cemetery.

But it all had to be done very quickly. The cameraman was already onsite on the 14th of September. To give added authenticity to the documentary, Tom Winter was to recount after the war [59], the Germans forced him, together with André Desgrange, to carry the bodies of their three comrades up above the high-tide mark, while the cameraman filmed the scene. The funeral took place the following day and the commanding officer had forbidden any civilians to take part in the ceremony[60], placing a dissuasive machine

---

[59] In Mike Langley's book, **Anders Lassen, VC, MC, of the SAS**, page 100.

gun 50 yards or so from the cemetery. However, he ordered that the head of the Gendarmerie brigade at Trévières be present in order to draft a report of the event to the French authorities. The entire ceremony was filmed.

From their hiding-place, a few of the village inhabitants were, nevertheless, able to get a glimpse of the procession and part of the ceremony. Never would the Germans have employed such luxury to honour the remains of British soldiers, had they not been offered this god sent opportunity to feed the Hitlerian propaganda programme.[61]

THE REACTION OF THE FRENCH AUTHORITIES

At the time, the French authorities had been slow to react. The Mayor of Saint-Laurent, M Feutry, an ex-bailiff, was officially informed of the attempted British landing by the Germans on the morning of the 13th of September. However, he judged it necessary to inform neither the Gendarmerie in Trévières, barely 5 miles away, nor the Sub-Prefect in Bayeux, 12 miles away. The head of the brigade in Trévières, Sergeant-Major

---

[60] According to certain second-hand sources, only the Mayor of Saint-Laurent and the village clerk were allowed to take part in the burial ceremony. This information is false, as proved by **the gendarmerie report dated 15th September 1942** and reproduced on the following pages.

[61] Unfortunately, no-one has been able to confirm to us that the film was in fact produced and broadcast in film theatres.

Léon, was only informed of the event at 19.00 hours. He finally finished his onsite investigation at 22.00 hours on the Sunday evening. By the time he reached the station, it was very late and he decided to wait till the following morning before advising his superior, Lieutenant Lepère, commander of the Gendarmerie in Bayeux. He did so between 08.30 and 09.00 hours.

The Lieutenant immediately informed the Sub-Prefect in Bayeux, Pierre Rochat, who, in turn, informed the Calvados Prefect, Michel Cacaud, in an all be it succinct written report addressed to the Prefect's Cabinet in the middle of the morning.

"14th September 1942
Dear Prefect of Calvados - Cabinet
I beg to inform you of an attempted landing that took place on the beach of Saint-Laurent-sur-Mer, at approximately 1.30 hours on the night of the 12th of September.
This attempt is said to have been carried out using 3 lightweight embarkations[62] one of which, made of canvas, remained wrecked on the beach.

---

[62] *This point of the report is false. The British commando only used two boats: the **MTB 344** and the **Goatley**, the large wooden, canvas and rubber vessel found by the Germans at low tide, overturned and wrecked. Neither the German reports with their appended maps, nor Geoffrey Appleyard's report mention a third vessel. The Sub-Prefect based his report on information received from the Trévières gendarmerie. It is evident that, for this precise point, his German source was false.*

The assailant losses are said to be 3 killed, 2 wounded and 2 prisoners.

I note that this information only reached me this Monday morning at 9.30 hours, the Gendarmerie Lieutenant only having, himself, been notified a few minutes earlier. I enclose a special report on the subject.

The funerals will take place on Tuesday 15ᵗʰ at 9.00 hours; German troops will pay homage.

I will take all the necessary measures to ensure that there be no incident.

The Sub-Prefect"

After the funeral ceremony, the head of the Trévières Gendarmerie, the only French authority present, drafted a report dated 15ᵗʰ September 1942,

"Trévières Brigade 15. 9. 42

Report by Sergeant-Major Léon, brigade commander.

On the burial of English soldiers at Saint-Laurent-sur-Mer.

The burial of English soldiers, killed at Saint-Laurent-sur-Mer, on the night of the 12ᵗʰ to the 13ᵗʰ of September took place today, at 09.00 hours, at the cemetery of the same village.

The three coffins, each covered with a sheaf of flowers, were placed on three wagons. They were preceded by the Company of German soldiers

stationed at Saint-Laurent-sur-Mer and followed by the officers.

At the cemetery, the ceremony was closed by a 3 gun salute.

No civilians took part in the ceremony; there was no incident.

The village authorities played no part in the organisation of the ceremony.

Signed: LEON"

This report was dispatched to the Sub-Prefect in Bayeux who, in turn, forwarded it to the Prefect's Cabinet on the 18th of September.

In a special report, the Prefect Cacaud rapidly informed his superior, the regional Prefect in Rouen, of the event, giving a brief summary of the previous reports made by the gendarmerie and the Bayeux Sub-Prefect,

"This attempt was made using three lightweight boats, one of which was of canvas and remained wrecked on the beach.

The three killed British soldiers were buried in Saint-Laurent cemetery on the 15th of September at 09.00 hours. The coffins were covered with flowers, preceded by a company of German soldiers stationed at Saint-Laurent and followed by officers.

No civilians.

At the cemetery, the ceremony ended with a three gun salute".

The *"British hit and run attack"* was again mentioned in the general information report that the Calvados Prefect sent, on the 4th of November 1942, to the Cabinet of the Head of State, to the Minister and Secretary of State for the Interior, to Foreign Affairs and to the Minister for Information, Pierre Laval in Vichy, as well as to the regional Prefect in Rouen,

> *"Caen, 4th November 1942*
> *Calvados Prefecture*
>
> *N°11*
> *Acts of war*
> *In the night of Saturday 12th to Sunday 13th of September, at approximately 02.00 hours, a British hit and run attack led by about thirty men, took place at Saint-Laurent-sur-Mer, in the Bayeux region.*
> *There were no victims among the French population. The assailants, who stayed on land for approximately one hour, lost three men. Furthermore, they left four men, two of whom were wounded, in the hands of the German troops.*
> *The dead were buried on the 15th of September without incident".*

The number of assailants mentioned in the prefectoral report is false. The error very probably originated from the Prefecture administration: but was it negligence on the part of a clumsy civil servant or a deliberate exaggeration for propaganda purposes? The error was so blatant (the genuine number of commandos, eleven men, being practically tripled), that we would tend to support the second theory.

From an administrative point of view the "Saint-Laurent affair" more or less ends there. Furious at having only been informed on the Monday morning, the Sub-Prefect Rochat requested that the Calvados Prefect take sanctions against the Mayor of Saint-Laurent and the head of the gendarmerie at Trévières,

"14th September 1942
Dear Prefect of Calvados - Cabinet

As I informed you in my report drafted today, the attempted British landing on the night of the 12th to the 13th of September was only brought to my attention on Monday 14th at 9.00 hours.

I immediately requested that the Mayor of Saint-Laurent explain himself, he who had not judged necessary to inform the gendarmerie of this event. This local magistrate, M Feutry, ex-bailiff, replied, "I had received no such orders", and since I expressed my astonishment, he added, "Is it me or you who should pay for the telephone call?" Before such infraction, and in view of M Feutry's attitude, I request that you take the necessary sanctions against him: either reprimand or dismissal. M Feutry had already demonstrated his ill-temper during a visit I made to his village. I was then obliged to severely call him to order.

The Gendarmerie Lieutenant will, in turn, take sanctions against the head of the Trévières brigade, who was aware of the attempted British landing on Sunday at 19.00 hours, and his enquiry having been completed at 22.00 hours, had awaited the following morning before informing the Sub-Prefect".

It would appear that the Sub-Prefect's request for sanctions went no further than a simple reprimand for the Mayor of Saint-Laurent, and we are unaware of any sanctions that may have been taken against the gendarme Léon.

Part three:

THE TRAGIC DESTINY OF CAPTAIN HAYES

Chapter I
Graham Hayes' great escape

We have, until now, deliberately omitted to mention one of the commando members, Captain Hayes, whose singular and exceptional experience in such circumstances, is worthy of a few personal chapters in this book.

If we cast our minds back, we can recall that Graham Hayes managed to re-embark the Goatley with his companions, all except Tony Hall who lay injured on the beach at Saint-Laurent. The vessel was immediately under enemy fire from German machine guns and sank when a nearby 75 mm gun positioned at WN 29c capsized it, casting all of its crew members overboard. How did Graham react at this crucial instant?

First of all, he was lucky enough not to have been injured, apart from an insignificant scratch on the left of his chin. He immediately rushed to help his Major March-Phillips who appeared to be in great difficulty. With all his strength, he endeavoured to carry him on his shoulder, but Gus gradually became completely inert. He was, undoubtedly, very seriously injured and had rapidly lost consciousness. With death in his soul, Graham had no choice but to abandon him. His own survival was at stake. Although he was an excellent swimmer, he very quickly gave up the idea of swimming back to the MTB which was already out of eye's sight. It is important to reconstitute these tragic instants of the raid, in order to fully appreciate Graham's achievement, as well as that of the three other commandos, Burton, Hellings and Orr who accomplished the same feat. The Germans were firing from all sides and sent many white, red and green rockets to illuminate the Saint-Laurent/Vierville sector.

To the west, the German defence appeared to be of lesser intensity, with the exception of a 75 mm cannon located on the beach at "Hamel au Prêtre" but busy firing out to sea towards the speed boat. Graham lost no time in disposing of his weapons, his waist belt, his shoes and anything else that might weigh him down or hinder his progression. On the beach at low tide, the Germans discovered five submachine guns, three waist belts with pistol and dagger and a bag containing two grenades.

After having hugged the shore until total exhaustion, Graham let the waves wash him up onto the beach before energetically crossing the sand to a hiding place. As soon as he had regained a little strength, he managed to find a passageway in the cliff, not far from "Hamel au Prêtre", in the vicinity of Vierville-sur-Mer. He advanced as best he could, despite his increasing fatigue, and progressed inland in a south-westerly direction. The moonless night and the hedgerows in that area of the Bessin district, which were far more abundant in 1942 than they are today, offered him protection.

As he approached the village of Asnières-en-Bessin, approximately 3 miles from the landing site, it was imperative that he find shelter before sunrise. He knew that the Germans would waste no time before scouring the beaches and the surrounding area. There was a farm at the village entrance. Graham decided to risk all and knocked on the front door. The household dog barked. A few moments later, the door opened and the farmer appeared. No need for the English officer to offer a detailed explanation. In any case, his limited knowledge of French would have prevented him from doing so. Marcel Lemasson immediately understood that he had before him a fleeing English soldier who was in difficulty. He had, like everyone else in the vicinity, heard the gunfire coming from Saint-Laurent beach a few hours earlier. So, he knew that an important event had taken place on the coast. The farmer welcomed Graham into his kitchen. The latter, immediately introduced himself, "Graham Hayes,

British officer", and requested, in words and in gestures, food, drink and some clean clothes. Without asking any questions, the farmer's wife rushed around in the kitchen to prepare him something hot to eat.

Marcel Lemasson, who didn't speak a word of English, was rather embarrassed. He talked to his wife and together they tried to determine how they could help this Englishman without risking his security and that of their own family. The Germans were omnipresent in the area. They would surely search the surrounding habitations until they found the fugitive. The farmer knew that any assistance offered to allied soldiers was severely punished. The Feldkommandantur regularly published reminders in the local newspaper columns. Before long, they decided to inform their neighbour, M de Brunville who was the local Mayor and who lived in the Château d'Asnières just across the road.

Shortly afterwards, Marcel Lemasson carefully closed the door behind him, calmed his dog in the yard, and carefully examined the approach to the farm and to the château. The small secondary road was deserted. Day had just dawned. He hurried towards the de Brunville's residence and entered into the courtyard via a discreet entrance.

The lord of the manor welcomed the farmer who hurriedly informed him of the presence of an English officer in his farm and asked him what he should do. Paul de Brunville immediately grasped the potential danger. The officer needed to be put into hiding as soon as possible in order to protect him from being tracked down by the Germans. His two children Olivier who was 22 and Isabelle, 20, both spoke English. He decided to go with his son to fetch the soldier and bring him back to the château. His wife was immediately informed but, since she had a leg injury, she was obliged to stay in bed throughout the adventure. With the utmost precaution, Olivier and his father brought Graham back from the farm as soon as evening fell. Isabelle observed from a first floor window. Stupor! Hardly had they entered into the château when a German patrol with a guard dog passed by; a close shave!

Shortly afterwards, Graham took quarters in the hay loft in the château's farm and, at nightfall, Olivier brought him food and drink. Finally dry and with a full stomach, Graham was then able to change from head to toe into civilian dress offered by Paul de Brunville before falling into a deep sleep.

Paul de Brunville, with his children, organised a genuine "war council" in the lounge of the château. How would they go about ensuring Captain Haye's safety and sending him back to England so that he could resume combat; such was the desire that the officer had so resolutely expressed to the de Brunville children? The only solution appeared to be to entrust him to the French Resistance. The Mayor of Asnières suddenly thought of his underwriter, Septime Humann,

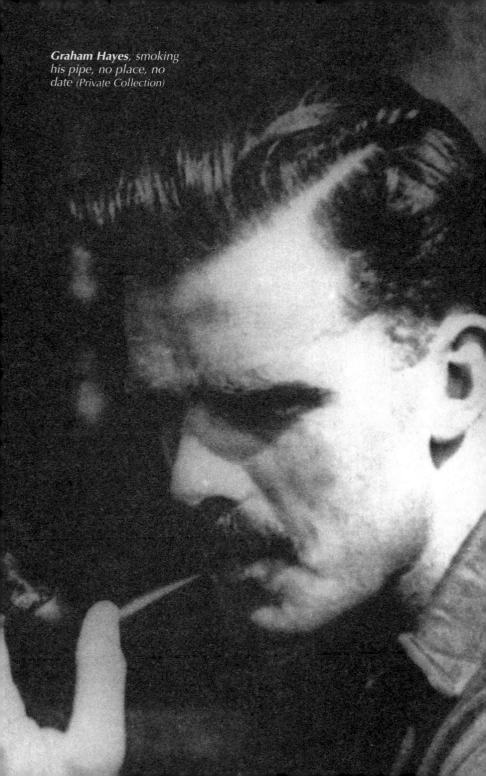

Graham Hayes, *smoking his pipe, no place, no date (Private Collection)*

Photograph of the château of the de Brunville family in Asnières-en-Bessin, where Graham Hayes was hidden. (Isabelle de Falandre Collection)

The de Brunville family ▶ in front of the Château of Asnières-en-Bessin. From left to right: Paul de Brunville, Olivier, his son, Isabelle, his daughter and Jeanne, his wife. October 1945. (Isabelle de Falandre Collection)

◀ Photograph taken at the rear of the de Brunville family château in Asnières-en-Bessin. To the right of the château, the barn where Graham Hayes was hidden. (Isabelle de Falandre Collection)

a WWI veteran who lived in Jouay-Mondaye. He was aware of his great patriotism and had every reason to suppose that he may well be a member of the Resistance, or if not, he was at least in contact with them. Olivier was to go to see him to seek advice the following morning.

On the 14th of September, the young man rang the doorbell at the underwriter's house; he was in fact the inspector for Normandy for the "Union et le Phénix Espagnol" insurance company. Alas, Mr Humann was bedridden that day; he was feverish due to anthrax in both legs. However, he promised Olivier de Brunville that he would take charge of the English captain the following morning; rendezvous at Bayeux railway station on the 9 o'clock train.

Among his fellow insurance agents, Septime Humann immediately thought of Suzanne Septavaux who lived in Le Pin, close to Moyaux in the Lisieux region. He knew her well for he had paid regular visits to her before the war during his rounds in the five Normandy departments. Approximately a year previously, she had joined a Resistance network organised by Dr Hautechaud, a general practitioner in Fervaques, a village situated 7 miles from Livarot. In the knowledge that she too desired to take action against the Occupant, he had asked her to join the network. His extensive business travel across Normandy had enabled him to collect a great deal of information on coastal defence, on rail and road traffic and on the German naval activities in the ports of Le Havre, Honfleur and Cherbourg. All such information was immediately forwarded to the central post in Paris and to London. Mme Septavaux lived alone with her nephew Emmanuel Des Georges, and the underwriter was sure that the officer would be safe with her while he sought the appropriate network to organise his escape to Spain, then to England via Gibraltar. Eight miles from Lisieux, her secluded house situated on the outskirts of the small village of Le Pin, with its mere 500 inhabitants, promised security and discretion and would be perfect for hiding the British officer.

When Olivier returned to Asnières, agitation was at its height. The secure transfer from the Bessin to the Pays d'Auge, two districts situated at opposite sides of Caen, needed to be organised. Graham Hayes was firstly to be taken to Bayeux station. There were no changes necessary on the Cherbourg - Paris train and Graham could travel direct to Lisieux. Septime Humann would then transport him from Lisieux station to Le Pin. Railway stations were dangerous places; the Germans were omnipresent, if not via their military attendance, at least by way of the personnel from the Reischbahn who doubled up with the SNCF staff. Identity controls were commonplace. They would have to play it tight. Olivier had given Mr Humann a description of Graham Hayes: a slim and tall man. He was to keep a close watch on him without entering into conversation. Olivier then explained to Graham that a 50-year old man, who he described in detail, would escort him from Bayeux to

Lisieux, from where he would take him to a female member of the Resistance, in a village not far from Saint Theresa's town.

They cycled from Asnières to Bayeux. Olivier cycled in front of Graham leaving a respectable distance between the two men. They arrived without incident at Bayeux railway station, but maintained a certain distance as if they were strangers. Olivier went to the counter and ordered a one-way second class ticket to Lisieux. At 8.30 am the railway platform was already bustling. However, amidst the crowd, Septime Humann had no difficulty in recognising the British officer whose looks and stature revealed his nationality, even to a short-sighted underwriter. Olivier had discreetly managed to give Graham the train ticket and he anxiously waited on the platform for the train to arrive from Cherbourg whilst glancing fretfully from time to time at Graham. The platform was teaming with German officers, all of them apparently at the height of exasperation. Was it the Saint-Laurent affair that had them in such a state? Luckily, none of them appeared to be preoccupied by that slim, fine man, whose thin moustache and brown combed back hair gave him the most British of allures. But then Olivier's worry turned to anxiety when he noticed four young men nudging at each other and designating Graham with a nod. Fortuitously, the express train was then announced on the crackling loud speaker, "*The train from Cherbourg and bound for Paris-Saint-Lazare is approaching platform two, ten minutes waiting*"

The young Olivier de Brunville observed the activity on the platform. The travellers were all motionless, their faces turned towards the right, where the steam train passed by the main station building and the first, then second class carriages came into sight. Septime climbed the steps up into one of the carriages to the rear of the train, followed close behind by Graham, to whom he had given a discreet hand signal. Grey-green uniforms were swarming. Cherbourg was a garrison town and many German troops were on leave. The two men stopped before the same compartment. Septime went inside to rest his weary legs. Graham stayed out in the corridor and engrossed himself in the **Bonhomme Normand**, a regional newspaper, that Septime had given him just before boarding the train. The express train left the station in a cloud of white smoke and a deafening clamour. Olivier had accomplished his mission with success. He was eager to return home to recount his adventure to the entire family, who impatiently and anxiously awaited his arrival.

The train journey from Bayeux to Caen was very short. At 9.30 am, the train left Caen and 45 minutes later, Saint Theresa's Cathedral was in view. Ticket control had been without incident. Septime Humann left the train. Graham followed. The station exit was free of any obstacle. The second phase of the transfer went just as smoothly as the first. All they now needed to ensure was the journey between Lisieux and Le Pin. The only obstacle would be the German guard at the town exit, next to the Citroen garage. On foot, the two men crossed the guard post with the most confounding ease. On such a Monday morning, the guards had no particular reason to be zealous. The short remaining distance between Lisieux and Le Pin proved to be problem free. However, Suzanne Septavaux had not yet been contacted and was unaware of their arrival. Septime had to ensure that she could in fact accommodate Graham, so, to avoid any unfortunate reaction, he hid him in a small wooded area not far from Le Pin and asked him to wait there. Only a few miles separated him from the Resistance house which he reached without difficulty.

Surprised to see her friend from Juaye-Mondaye arriving unexpectedly and on foot at her doorstep, Mme Septavaux welcomed him with warmth and much curiosity. Her nephew, Emmanuel, was present. They both listened with enthusiasm to Septime's account of the events since the 12th of September, or at least what Olivier de Brunville had told him: the landing of a British commando at Saint-Laurent-sur-Mer that had turned sour, the "salvage" of Captain Hayes, and finally his transfer to Le Pin into hiding, whilst awaiting an escape plan. Half an hour later, Septime Humann and Emmanuel Des Georges left to collect Graham in his hiding place to take him back to Suzanne Septavaux's house. Everything had gone smoothly. The British officer was in good hands. Graham was reassured and confident for the future. He now needed to rest to gain the necessary strength for the trials yet to come.

CHAPTER II
GRAHAM HAYES AND THE
JEAN-MARIE/DONKEYMAN NETWORK

Two weeks after his arrival at Le Pin, Graham Hayes fell ill and was bed-ridden. The goat's cheese he had eaten at the end of his meal had not been sufficiently refrigerated. Suzanne Septavaux called Dr Hautechaud from Fervaques, who, after examining Graham, diagnosed Maltese fever. He was also suffering from knee pains; his meniscus had been operated on prior to the Saint-Laurent raid which had revived this previous injury. Graham was therefore confined to bed for several weeks.

The network that Paul Hautechaud had created himself at the beginning of 1941, had initially attracted members with strong personalities who, without really knowing how to go about it, sought to combat the presence of a foreign army on French soil. Earnest patriots, they observed, listened and passed on information to the head of the network. Henri Beaudet, a farmer from Notre-Dame-de-Courson, was among the network's first members. With a handful of trustworthy friends, he formed a small embryonic Resistance group in the vicinity of Orbec-Livarot. Suzanne Septavaux and her nephew were also among the first members of the Resistance in this Calvados district.

The network was strongly established in Lisieux throughout the first six months of 1942. Dr Hautechaud had entrusted the responsibility of this sector to Roland Bloch, one of his son's ex schoolmates from the Marcel Gambier High School, whose pseudonym was Hugo. He was an insurance agent who had been recommended by Mme Septavaux. The Lisieux group rapidly developed when Hautechaud himself recruited M Delaunay, a bookseller in rue Pont-Mortain, who in turn, a short while later, ensured the active participation of Minister Orange and his wife Hélène, who lived in Rue Guizot. The minister, in turn, recruited one of his parishioners, Robert Stalhand, a farmer from La Brévière, then Stalhand's friend François-Xavier De Maistre, a cattle merchant from Saint-Martin-du-Mesnil-Oury and a practicing Catholic. In Lisieux, the network could also count on Maurice Fromont, ex-Reserve Lieutenant now employed at the town's funeral parlour, and on his friend Jean Grignola, a heating fitter from 36 Boulevard Sainte-Anne. Grignola was related to the Cabioch family who had a fruit and vegetable store in Rue Pierre Colombe, since his sister Jeannette had married the youngest of their three sons, Joseph. During a family meal, Jean Grignola had sounded out Olivier, the eldest of the three, who later accepted to join the network. The Saint-Désir-de-Lisieux haberdashery, run by Gaëtane Bouffay, a parishioner from the Reformed Church in Lisieux, was the network's letterbox and occasional meeting place. The early autumn contacts were promising and it was hoped that there would be rapid extension towards the north of the Pays d'Auge, and in particular on the coast. In May, Dr Hautechaud received a visit from Robert Kieffer, alias *Raoul*, an ex-member of the Interallié network, the best part of which had been broken up late 1941, early 1942 by the Abwehr, the Wehrmacht's counterespionage service. Kieffer had joined André Girard's network, codenamed "Carte", but had received orders from his right-hand man, Paul, an architect whose real name was Jacques Henri Frager. This ex-Reserve Captain from the Engineers was preparing to set out for London to obtain material and financial support. Paul had commissioned *Raoul* to act as a link between the Normandy groups and Paris; in other words to transmit collected information together with the Parisian central post's directives.

Dr Hautechaud met regularly with *Raoul* and informed him of recent developments in the Pays d'Auge sector. Hence, in September 1942, he informed him of the presence of a British officer, the survivor of a failed raid to the west of Port-en-Bessin, who was in hiding at Le Pin. Paul had already returned from his trip to London on the 20th of July, by felucca, and was accompanied by two agents from the Special Operations Executive (SOE), Commander Nicholas Bodington and Yvonne Rudelat; they had come to France to check out the Carte organisation. On their return to England, the British officer gave a report of their visit to his superior officer, Colonel Maurice Buckmaster who was in charge of the "F" section of the SOE, giving a very positive appraisal of the network's activity. The British information services were so satisfied that on the 28th of August 1942, André Girard, the organisation's national head, obtained the expedition of a British officer (Captain Peter Churchill) and a radio-operator (Captain Adolphe Rabinovitch) in order to facilitate the liaison with London.

Hence, much to his ignorance, the SSRF commando Captain Hayes, responsible to Combined Operations, but more particularly to the SOE, had been taken in by a Resistance network controlled by the very same SOE. It was only in March 1943, when Girard handed it over to Frager, that the network was codenamed "Jean-Marie", another of Frager's pseudonyms. The French section of the SOE then assigned it to the "Buckmaster networks" under the codename "Donkeyman Circuit".

Dr Hautechaud, who was one of the rare Frenchmen in the region authorised to use his own vehicle, paid weekly visits to Graham Hayes at Le Pin. Born in Bordeaux, this 46-year old practitioner had moved to Fervaques with his wife Andrée and their two children in the early 1920's. Paul Hautechaud very quickly found his place among the 600 inhabitants of the Norman village. An active man, he very rapidly invested himself in local activities including the Sports Association for which he was chairman from 1926 to 1928. He then handed over the chairmanship to fully commit himself to the Veterans Society. He was a Reserve Captain and had served during the First World War. In 1931, he accepted the position of Vice-chairman and remained so until 1938.

He was a small man, with a high forehead and brown combed back hair; his eyes, sparkling with a blend of intelligence and malice, observed with surprising intensity from behind his small round spectacles. Every one of his traits, his expression, his gestures and his dignified allure were the personification of courage and determination. It didn't take him long to be elected onto his village council, from 1926 when he replaced a resigning councillor, and to again obtain a seat in the 1929 local elections. Graham appreciated his visits. From his bedroom window, he watched him arrive in his Simca, via the muddy track that separated the secondary road from Mme Septavaux's house, his pipe permanently wedged between his lips. This detail immediately appealed to Graham who was, himself, a great amateur of pipe smoking. Their conversations often turned to comparing different qualities of pipe or the varying aromas of English and French tobacco. Another detail that the British officer had noted was the fineness of the practitioner's hands; slim and neat, almost like those of a lady, they were in constant movement when he spoke, as if to add strength to his words. When he examined his knee, changing its position, checking his articulations and his meniscus, Graham was surprised by the force contained in those delicate little hands.

Suzanne Septavaux and her nephew, Emmanuel Des Georges often took part in their discussions with great interest and Graham had, of course, accepted to recount the events leading to and following the Aquatint raid on Saint-Laurent beach. He, naturally, evoked the personality of some of his comrades, starting with his superior, Major March-Phillips, whom everyone at the SSRF was used to calling Gus, and who was spoken of with great respect and consideration. Inevitably, and with great affection, and even certain tenderness, almost tangible in his tone of voice, Graham spoke of his childhood friend Apple, Geoffrey Appleyard. In his best, but rather poor French, Graham explained that their families were from the same Yorkshire village, Linton-on-Wharfe, near Wetherby and York, and that they were close friends. As his thoughts went out to the young and intrepid 25-year old, his ordinarily serious and almost melancholic expression turned to a gentle smile. Geoffrey had gone to great pains to convince Gus to let him take part in operation Aquatint and the compromise had finally been that he should stay on the motorboat as second in command. What had become of Appleyard? Had he managed to safely return to England? Graham often wondered.

The possible answers brought with them further interrogations and, one day, Graham accepted to talk about his family. With great emotion, he spoke firstly of his mother, Lilian Grace, a very pious woman full of kindness and exceptionally proud of her five children, and for whom Graham had the most profound affection. He had inherited from his father, Herbert Charles, his taste for action and adventure as well as his passion for wood carving. Graham continued and described, in turn, each of his brothers; Denis the eldest at 33 who had been very close to Graham since their childhood; Malcolm, aged 23 who was a Lieutenant in a bomber unit and of whom Graham appreciated the self-control and "daredevil" nature; his youngest brother, Austen, 22, who, before he enlisted, had helped Graham to close his sculpture workshop in Temple Sowerby and whose greatest desire was to work with his elder brother as a carpenter and cabinetmaker; and finally Graham described his younger sister.

After three weeks rest, Graham was on the way to recovery. He was already able to leave his room and

Suzanne Septavaux's house in Le Pin, where Graham was hidden from the 15th of September to the 20th of October. Photograph taken in 2004.

▲
Tapestry embroidered by Graham Hayes during his stay at Mme Suzanne Septavaux's house in Le Pin from the 15th of September to the 20th of October 1942. (Private collection)

◀ *Portrait of Dr Paul Hautechaud taken by Koch, a Lisieux photographer. January 1937. (Private collection)*

take a walk in the garden. To occupy the long autumn evening, he took to embroidery. He had seen Suzanne Septavaux embroider the tapestries of several dimensions that adorned the walls of her living room. So, following his "guardian angel's" advice, he took a small 15cm square of canvas and set to work. When he had completed his work of art, Graham was far from disappointed by the result. He had embroidered a side-on view of a German soldier in uniform with helmet, belts and boots and holding in hishand, just below his Hitlerian moustache, a red flower. A swastika was perfectly visible on his helmet and left no doubt as to his nationality. Behind him, what we suppose to be a ram was ready and waiting to charge the soldier's somewhat protruding posterior. Graham maliciously represented himself in the symbolic form of a crow observing the scene from the branch of a tree in blossom.

Six weeks after his arrival, Dr Hautechaud came to visit Graham to discuss, one last time, his departure. It had all been arranged with *Raoul*. Graham would, first of all, be taken to Paris and handed over to another of the network's agents who would await the most propitious moment to take him by train to the Pyrenean Mountains together with other stowaways. A Resistance border escort would then help him cross the Spanish border, from where he was to make his own way to the British Consulate in Madrid. From then on, things would surely go smoothly for all he needed to do was to reach Gibraltar from where he would be repatriated to England.

Graham was suddenly filled with emotion. But not because of the many risks he would now have to face during his long journey to Spain: the Gestapo, the hazardous crossing of the Pyrenean Mountains, the Guardia Civil... No, the young officer was suddenly submerged by his immense gratitude to all of these men and women who, so undemanding and so obliging, ran the most tremendous of risks, simply by keeping him in hiding. Before his arrival in Asnières, then in Le Pin, Graham knew nothing of the French Resistance. He had, of course, heard of a handful of patriots who dared to defy the prohibitions set by the Occupant; however, he had no real knowledge of how they operated. He had no idea that the Resistance was an emerging force, a fundamental movement comprising men and women of all ages, of all origins, of all social backgrounds and of all political, philosophical and religious convictions. Emmanuel Des Georges, with whom he had so often talked during these long weeks, had opened his eyes. As a sales representative, he easily obtained the necessary passes to travel within forbidden zones. He had therefore been able to approach the coastal defence at Port-en-Bessin and to convey information to *Raoul* that was of undeniable military importance. Graham promised himself that, as soon as he reached England, he would draft a detailed report informing his superiors of the infinitely precious role of the Resistance in the common battle against Nazism.

Emmanuel had just confirmed that Graham's departure was planned for the following week, on Tuesday the 20th of October. Paul Hautechaud would come to fetch him and would take him to Lisieux. Suzanne would go with them. She was to wait with Graham on Thiers Square in front of the cathedral, before handing him over to *Raoul* and another agent from Paris. They were then to take the train with him to Saint-Lazare in Paris, thus ensuring his protection.

On the Monday evening after dinner, it was time for farewells. As a reminder of his "convalescence", Graham offered Suzanne his canvas, patiently embroidered throughout these long weeks of forced rest which had enabled him to regain enough strength to continue his way home. He promised he would write soon and that, as soon as he made his way back to England, he would send her a personal message on the BBC airwaves. Graham's suitcase was quickly filled and fastened. On the morning of the 20th, Paul Hautechaud arrived in front of the house in his Simca which was now quite familiar to Graham. Emotion was at its height and throats were tight. Graham sat in the front passenger seat. Suzanne sat in the back. Very few words were spoken throughout the journey. Paul Hautechaud appeared nervous, despite his efforts to appease the atmosphere. The small car soon arrived in front of the cathedral. The doctor vigorously shook

Graham's hand before hurrying off. He had better not be seen here at such an early hour.

Suzanne and Graham waited on the square for *Raoul* and his companion to arrive. The Lisieux streets were barely starting to rouse. Saint Peter's church chimed 8 am. Graham's train was due to leave in an hour; the Parisian agent shouldn't be long now. 8.30 am. Suzanne became anxious. If *Raoul* didn't arrive in the next five to ten minutes, they were surely going to miss the 9 o'clock train. What could she do? Hindering on the square represented an increasing risk; they were likely to be spotted. Suzanne sent Graham off to the cathedral and told him to stay close to the entrance where she could easily give him a discreet wave as soon as she saw *Raoul*. 9 am. The express train for Paris had left Lisieux railway station. Suzanne was frantic. What had gone wrong? Why was *Raoul* not there? Graham had gone inside the cathedral and was sitting in the nave. He prayed for a while. Outside, the traffic had gradually become more and more intense. Tuesday was market day. The church bells chimed 9.30. Suzanne rushed to fetch Graham. She had just distinguished *Raoul* at the corner of Rue Pont-Mortain and Rue Henry Chéron. The two men apologised profusely. They had missed their train from Saint-Lazare and had taken the following one. Suzanne was evidently furious. Graham, rather embarrassed, remained silent. Luckily, another express train was due to leave Lisieux at 10.27 am. Suzanne hurriedly kissed the English officer goodbye and wished him good luck. For a moment, she watched the three men walk off energetically towards Rue d'Alençon which would lead them to the railway station, before, herself, turning off into Rue Henry Chéron to leave Lisieux and return home to Le Pin.

Suzanne Septavaux and her Resistance leader, Paul Hautechaud were both totally oblivious to the fact that they had just handed Graham over to the Abwehr, the German army's formidable counterespionage service.

Chapter III
Raoul's Betrayal

During the train journey, Graham Hayes had no idea of what was in store. The two men who had taken seat in the same compartment inspired him with confidence, particularly *Raoul*, whose jovial expression and mocking smile immediately put his companions at ease.

The second man, Robert Goubeau, alias *Bob*, appeared perhaps to be slightly less forthcoming, but it was no doubt due to the stress and the vexation caused by their missed morning rendezvous, together with the fatigue of the journey from Paris to Lisieux. It was now midday. Kieffer and Goubeau nudged each other. They simultaneously pulled out of their pockets two meagre sandwiches for which they had paid a relative fortune at the Lisieux railway station buffet just before leaving. Shortly afterwards, Graham, without uttering a word, did the same. *Don't speak. Act as if you are perfect strangers.* Such were the orders they had been given.

Kieffer devoured his paltry meal in no time. He gazed nonchalantly at the sweeping landscape. At that time of year, the green meadows of the Normandy countryside were rich in colour and the orchards over-flowing with apple trees laden with the burden of their maturing harvest. He was familiar with the Saint-Lazare - Caen - Cherbourg line for having taken it so many times since the beginning of the war; ever since Armand, the head of the Interallié network, had entrusted him with the mission of federating the first Resistance groups in the Manche region and contacting those they could join forces with in Calvados.

With his eyes half shut, lulled by the monotonous and juddering sound of the train running at high speed, the Abwehr agent appeared to be immersed in thought. What was the use in dredging all that up again? But the desire was overwhelming. Just like a film that he watched, rewound and watched again, he recalled his every step since the beginning of the war.

An ex-Air Force Flight Sergeant, he had been affected to the 33rd Air Squadron based in Nancy in 1934, after training at the Ecole de Pilotage d'Ambérieux, pilot school in the Ain region. In 1937, he had returned to civilian life and was employed as an engineer at the Tuileries Mécaniques de Champignolles in the Côte-d'Or region. Remobilised in 1938, he briefly fought in the Ardennes with the Groupe d'Observateurs Aérien 2/250, aerial observer group, during the German offensive. In June 1940, he had withdrawn to Perpignan and had then embarked for La Sénia, an airbase in Oran, in Algeria. In September 1940, he was demobilised with the rank of Flight Sergeant and regained his native village of Moncel-sur-Seille in the Meurthe-et-Moselle region, rejoining his mother who had been widowed in December 1938.

Kieffer was not the kind of man likely to languish in this insignificant Lorraine village. In December 1940, he made an important decision: he would travel to England via North Africa. On foot, he managed to clandestinely cross the demarcation line at Cormery in the Indre-et-Loire region and then made his way to Marseille. Thanks to a naval construction engineer, who was perfectly aware of his intentions, he obtained a job in the harbour thus enabling him to wait for the first opportunity to board a vessel heading for Algeria. However, his efforts were in vain, for the harbour was kept under close surveillance by the Armistice Commission officers.

His commitment to the Resistance began, one evening in January 1941, when he met Armand in a bar in Rue Beauvau, not far from Marseille's Old Port. Kieffer was later to learn that Armand was an officer, a fighter pilot in the Polish Army, and a graduate from the Warsaw Superior War School. He had also trained for two months at the Ecole de Guerre in Paris. His real name was Captain Roman Czerniawski.[63] He had asked Kieffer to work for one of the very first Resistance networks in the non-occupied zone. He had initially baptised the network: the Family or F2[64], and the British were later to rename it Interallié, since it was a Franco-Polish network. Kieffer's first mission was to collect information on port activity: ship movements and defensive military installations.

[63] *According to the book by Oscar Reile,* **Geheime Westfront,** *Verlag Welsermühl, München und Wels, 1962, translated into French by R. Jouan, under the title:* **L'Abwehr, Le contre-espionnage allemand en France,** *preface by Colonel Rémy, Editions France-Empire, 1970,* **Roman Czerniawski** *had come to France after his country's defeat, and had managed to enlist in the French Army. In Lunéville, during the winter of 1939-1940, he had met a pretty young woman called Renée Borni who had fallen passionately in love with him. She was later to provide him with false identity papers, originally held by her deceased husband, Armand Borni. It was hence that Captain Roman Czerniawski was to be known as* **Armand.**

[64] *By July 1940, Czerniawski had set up his first network in Toulouse, together with two other Polish officers,* **Zarembski** *(pseudo* **Tudor***) and* **Slowikowski** *(pseudo* **Ptak***); network that was to be named "Family" or "F2". Early 1941, with derisory resources, the three men recruited 250 agents, 40 of whom were Polish. "F2" established rapid contact with the British secret services and constituted an information service of which* **Armand,** *as an Air Force Captain, was to develop the "aviation" branch throughout the occupied zone. He consequently recruited several officers and non-commissioned officers from the Air Force. After having handed the network over to W. Krzysanowki (pseudo* **Panhard***),* **Armand** *headed for Paris, in early November 1940, to found, together with* **the Cat,** *the "PO Paris" network. (This information is taken from Part I of* **l'Histoire de la Résistance en France, juin 1940-juin 1941** *under the auspices of Henri Noguères, Robert Laffont, Paris, 1967, which we invite the reader to consult for more detailed information).*

There was also a woman, Armand's mistress. She was small with jet black hair and an expression of such disturbing beauty that everyone in the network called her La Chatte, the Cat. Her name was in fact Mathilde Carré, but she was also known as Micheline.

Armand had rapidly seized Kieffer's immense potential, to such an extent that he included him in the management team in Paris where he personally, together with the Cat, developed the network within the occupied zone. He had initially asked Kieffer to go to the Manche region to give a certain Lucien a hand in recruiting. The ex air force Flight Sergeant, who hid his true identity behind his pseudonym of *Raoul*, very soon proved to be of such surprising efficiency that he was given the responsibility of the "D" sector, thus replacing Lucien who had been arrested. He was therefore in charge of the two Normandy regions: Manche and Calvados.

As such, Kieffer did remarkable and intelligent work for the Interallié network, however his greatest desire was to reach England and to fly again, this time for the Royal Air Force. On several occasions, he had confided in Armand, however the latter would have none of his adventure stories and repeated to him that he was of far more use to the allied cause in France than he ever would be in England. But his chief finally agreed to let Kieffer return to Marseille, and gave him the necessary contacts to make his way to Spain.

In a café in Argelès-sur-Mer, he managed to find a guide who promised to add him to an already overloaded group of stowaways. The long and laborious crossing of the Pyrenean Mountains had gone relatively well, however the imprudent group was arrested in Figueras by the Spanish carabineers. After having been thrown in jail, they were finally taken back to the border and handed over to the French authorities at the Col du Perthus. In the town of Ceret, in the Oriental Pyrenees, Kieffer was condemned by the court to one month's imprisonment and he served his sentence in Perpignan prison. Kieffer had been relatively lucky, all things considered, and he managed to make his way back to Marseille, then to Paris at the end of June 1941.

By the beginning of the summer months, *Raoul* had resumed his return journeys between the French capital and Normandy. In the Manche, he had worked well. He had recruited several agents including Marie-Thérèse Buffet, née Fillon, who was to become his main contact during his regular trips to Cherbourg at the beginning of each month. She collected and centralised the information provided by the twenty regional agents: fishermen, labourers, policemen, railwaymen, a chemist and young women and girls. Equipment, maps, information sheets, reports on the Kommandantur, on staff, on the German defence positions (coastal batteries, Flak, concrete shelters), on units, on types of ship used, their armaments and their mooring positions, etc., all such information was delivered to 25 Rue Val de Saire in Cherbourg. It was the network's letterbox, but it was also the place of residence of Mme Bertrand, also known as Marie-Thérèse Buffet, who assembled the rich harvest before handing it over to *Raoul*. *Raoul*, in turn, had the documents forwarded to Armand via another letterbox situated at the "La Palette" café in the Montparnasse quarter in Paris.

It was with a certain dose of nostalgia that Robert Kieffer recalled that short period during which he had worked for the Resistance and for the allied cause with fervour and conviction. However, everything took a different turn when Marie-Thérèse Buffet took it upon herself to recruit sub-agents, including a certain Emile Lemeur, whom she had met purely by chance in a shelter during a bombing alert. Emile Lemeur had previously worked for the Cherbourg town council and his appearance, his face ravaged by alcohol, did not exactly inspire confidence. But the key to his recruitment in the Resistance was the fact that he worked in one of the Luftwaffe's fuel depots. The problem with Emile Lemeur was that he talked too much, far too much, particularly after a day's work when he paid his usual visit to his favourite bistro. One evening in the month of October, the 18th to be precise, perhaps a little more inebriated than usual, he started to chat with a Corporal from the German Air Force and he told him the most curious things: a woman had asked him some weird questions about the depot, where the barrels of fuel were sent, what type of plane was used, and many more questions to which he was unable to reply. The Corporal nodded, and with much astonishment, took careful note of every detail of their conversation. As soon as he left the drunkard, he immediately informed his superiors. Then one thing leading to another, the affair finally made its way to the head of the local Geheime Feld Polizei (GFP), the German secret field police, which was in fact one of the Abwehr's executory organs. Two days later, the superintendent of the Cherbourg GFP informed the III-F section of the Abwehr based in Saint-Germain-en-Laye and headed by Lieutenant Colonel Oscar Reile. Within the section, there was a smaller unit, the Referat III f, led by Commander Esching who was specifically in charge of counterespionage and the preservation of secrets.

Commander Esching was convinced that this was the first major espionage affair that the unit would have to deal with and he immediately sent Captain Erich Borchers to Cherbourg. After a few days surveillance of Marie-Thérèse Buffet's home, the Abwehr officer arrested her[65] thanks to Lemeur who had readily

---

[65] **Marie-Thérèse Buffet** was deprted to Ravensbrück concentration camp, under the category "N.N." (**Nacht und Nebel**, "Night and Fog"), in other words the detainees destined, as per the ordinances signed on the 7th of December 1941 by Field Marshal Keitel, head of the OKW organisation, to disappear within the nebulous concentration camp system without leaving a trace. She joined the evacuation convoy on the 2nd of March 1945 towards Mauthausen concentration camp in Austria, where she was registered under the new number 1381. Marie-Thérèse Buffet returned home from deportation.

revealed the address and a physical description of Mme Bertrand. Inside the house, a harvest of information on the secret organisation, well beyond Captain Borcher's wildest dreams, was unveiled. The Interallié linchpin had found no better than to keep "*genuine packets of reports and information given by the agents and drafted on sorts of sheets, together with other maps with abundant information; in short, material enabling us to draw consequential conclusions as to the enemy information service's operations*".[66] wrote Borchers in a later report.

However, the most dramatic discovery, for the network, was the entire list of the Manche agents, found under the living room rug by one of the German soldiers. Throughout the first week of November, the GFP arrested, one after another, a fisherman from Barfleur together with his daughters aged 16 and 20; Jeanne Frigout[67], a 19-year old student in Saint-Lô; her uncle, Auguste Mabire[68], a pilot in Granville harbour; a

[66] Translated from Major Borchers, **Abwehr contre Résistance**, Amiot-Dumont, Paris, 1949, pages 19-20.

[67] We invite readers to consult the account by **Jeanne Frigout,** later **Jeanne Ferrès**, in the special edition of **Liberté-Le Bonhomme Libre**, June 1994, pages 48-49. Arrested on the 6th of November 1941, Jeanne Frigout was placed in confinement, for 11 months at the Santé Prison in Paris, for 10 months at Fresnes Prison, then for a short period at Romainville fort, before being deported to Ravensbrück (POW n° 21 670), in the "N.N." category. She was liberated in April 1945 and repatriated via Sweden on the 26th of June 1945.

[68] Arrested in Granville on the 7th of November 1941, **Auguste Mabire** was imprisoned at Cherche-midi Prison in Paris and was released after one year.

pharmacy assistant, Maurice Lebos[69], in Les Pieux; Angèle Gallie, shop assistant in Cherbourg, Georges Herbert, lorry driver[70], etc…

After being arrested, Kieffer had learned all of this from the very mouth of the man who was to become his chief for the rest of the Occupation: a non-commissioned officer from the Wehrmacht, Sergeant Hugo Bleicher. Captain Borchers, who did not speak French, had requested an interpreter. It was hence that, he who was to become one of the Abwehr's best men, entered for the first time into the whole story. But let us read the words written by Bleicher himself, in his accurate recollection of his first meeting with Captain Borchers.

"On the 23rd of October 1941, the date is engraved in my memory; I had replaced the superintendent in the department in Rue de l'Amiral Courbet. Meanwhile, I had obtained the rank of non-commissioned officer; however I was still an auxiliary policeman and interpreter. That evening, I was sitting reading my reports and totally oblivious to what was going on. Suzanne had just called us to dinner, when a man in a tattered raincoat with a green hat, apparently in a great hurry and quite discontented, burst into the

---

[69] **Maurice Lebos** was deported to Germany under the category "N.N." to Sarrebrück-Neue Bremme, then to Dachau (n°50548), Dora and Bergen-Belsen, from where he was liberated on the 15th of April 1945.

[70] **Georges Herbert** was deported to Mauthausen concentration camp (n°25512), and died on the 16th of May 1943 in Gusen.

room without knocking. He immediately introduced himself, without any further formality, as a captain from the AST at Saint-Germain. I was dumbfounded. Until then, I had nurtured a quite different idea of what an officer from the Abwehr might look like. But this tall, slim man of around 50, who in no way resembled an officer, appeared to know exactly what he wanted".[71]

As usual, Kieffer had taken the midday train from Saint-Lazare on that 3rd of November 1941. The journey was without incident and the train arrived in Cherbourg at the planned arrival time of 15.30 hours. He was first of all surprised, but only a little, to see Lemeur waiting for him in the hall. He knew that the corpulent Lemeur had somewhat irregular working hours. However, at the station exit, hardly had he made twenty paces when two sturdy brutes grabbed him from under the arms and literally threw him into a darkened vehicle. Rapidly handcuffed, he found himself between two Germans in civilian dress: Borchers and Bleicher; he was only to learn their identity some time later. However, he had grasped that the same fate had awaited Lemeur in the vehicle that followed.

After a speedy interrogation at Fortress Cherbourg, Kieffer could clearly remember, for it was only a year

[71] *"Erich Borchers, Sergeant Bleicher, Monsieur Jean", Adolf Sponholz Editions , Hanover, page 27.*

ago, he was driven to Cherche-Midi prison in Paris in the evening. The real interrogation started on the following morning, under the skilful control of M Jean, who was no other than Bleicher himself.

The German had immediately put his cards on the table. Lemeur had identified him, at Cherbourg station, as being the regional chief in charge of Resistance liaisons with Paris. When he was searched after being arrested, notes on German military installations in Calvados had been found, together with several coded messages. In Marie-Thérèse Buffet's house, the entire list of the Manche agents had been found and they were all, already or soon to be, imprisoned. It was clear that there was no point whatsoever in denying his involvement with a Resistance network for which they already possessed substantial information, and would no doubt continue to collect more throughout their numerous perquisitions and interrogations. However, Kieffer was far from talkative, thus giving himself time to think, an attitude that was to cost him two weeks confinement in a dilapidated cell of that sinister Parisian prison.

Hugo Bleicher awaited his hour. He would wait for the fruit to be ripe before harvesting. The non-commissioned officer revelled in the anticipation. He was finally given the opportunity to fully exploit his potential in the Abwehr where he had been freshly recruited. From his transfer into the GFP commando at the beginning of March 1941, until Lemeur's arrest in Cherbourg, he had been particularly bored. Luckily, his girlfriend, Suzanne Renouf, whom he had met at the "Pelican" bar in Caen in August 1940, had accepted to follow him to Saint-Lô the following month, and then to Cherbourg. He had acquired his perfect knowledge of French during the First World War after having been taken prisoner at Verdun and detained in an internment camp in Abbeville. This new proficiency had opened the doors of an unknown and hazardous world, that of the clandestine battle against an invisible but formidable enemy, an enemy who had not yet been given the name "Resistance".

After the war, his superior, Captain Erich Borchers had given a very accurate portrait of Bleicher, "*That man with black spectacles who never opens his mouth. I had initially recruited him as an interpreter at the GFP, but I rapidly realised that he had the potential to become an unrivalled auxiliary for our department. He is extraordinarily intelligent, with nerves of steel; he is a cold calculating man who never misjudges emotion. From behind his dark glasses, he is capable of reading the most secret of thoughts and men become as malleable as wax in his hands. He never drinks alcohol but consumes alarming quantities of coffee and smokes the most pungent cigarettes. A tireless worker, fatigue has no effect on him. I have never heard him utter a single word of a private nature. Bastian (Bleicher) speaks perfect French and appears to know all of the dialects*".[72]

---

[72] Translated from **Major Borchers**, opus cit., pages 20-21.

Kieffer had initially underestimated Bleicher who had led him to believe that Marie-Thérèse Buffet had betrayed him through jealousy. Cut to the quick, revolted even, Kieffer had revenged himself by explaining in detail the role played by Marie-Thérèse Buffet in the organisation of the Interallié network, thus confirming information that the German policeman already had in his possession. Then, completely exhausted, he had confined himself to obstinate and resigned silence. Days went by. Bleicher would visit less frequently for a while, before returning to the attack, regularly changing his tactics. He spoke to Kieffer without hounding him, almost on an equal man-to-man basis, highlighting that the Abwehr knew everything about the network's activities and that his chiefs were only waiting for the right time to arrest every last one of its members. By giving Bleicher the few missing parts to the puzzle, Kieffer would save his skin. Where were Armand's letterboxes? That was all he wanted to know. He asked him for no names. He believed Kieffer when he told him that he was oblivious to Armand's hiding place. He just wanted to ensure the recovery of all of the mail that had been sent to him. The ex Flight Sergeant could feel himself weakening. After all, mail was never signed and messages were always coded.

Kieffer finally gave in to the policeman's incessant and exigent demands and revealed the addresses of two letterboxes, one at the "La Palette" café and one at

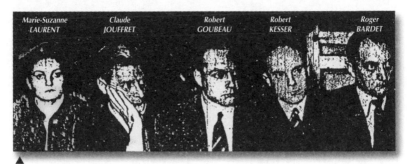

| Marie-Suzanne | Claude | Robert | Robert | Roger |
| LAURENT | JOUFFRET | GOUBEAU | KESSER | BARDET |

Photograph of Robert Kieffer (second from the right with an erroneous surname) together with his co-defendants. Photograph taken during their trial in 1949, and published in the Aurore daily newspaper's 6ᵗʰ December 1949 issue.

the Berlitz School, close to the Place de l'Opéra. Had he realised? By giving the address of the latter, he had seriously endangered the lives of Armand and the Cat who paid regular visits there. The Abwehr agent immediately had the two locations placed under discreet surveillance.

Bleicher then decided to take the bull by the horns. After two weeks of confinement,of Kieffer was beginning to falter. He was in dreadfully low spirits. Bleicher was well aware. With the most infinite precaution, he suggested to his prisoner that he work for the Abwehr, in other words for the German counterespionage service, whose activities and methods, he reassured him, were far from those employed by the Gestapo!

Kieffer clearly remembered that crucial moment. It was precisely on the 14ᵗʰ of November that he was to make a dramatic volte-face, agreeing finally to cross the line and to work for the enemy. Freedom, easy money, his predilection for risk and adventure, it was all just too tempting. After lengthy consideration and after having obtained the solemn promise that none of the network's members would be referred to a German military court to be condemned to death and executed, (which took a great weight off Kieffer's conscience) he finally accepted Bleicher's proposal.

On the same day, or perhaps on the 15th of November, he was no longer sure, Kieffer, was free and had met with Claude Jouffret at the Berlitz School letterbox where he had asked him to fix a rendezvous with Armand on the 16th of November from 14.00 to 15.00 hours at the "La Palette" café in the Montparnasse quarter in Paris. However, Jouffret was too busy and, instead of going to see Armand himself, he sent one of his liaison officers, Christian, a Polish officer. Kieffer had insisted that he must meet with Armand in person, for he needed to set up a maritime liaison with England. Christian took this new and somewhat vague request to the Interallié chief. Armand sent him back to see Kieffer with a list of precise questions concerning the liaison. Bleicher, who had observed every last detail of the exchange, then decided to arrest the liaison officer. However, Christian remained silent despite repeated threats and physical violence.

Sinking a little deeper into betrayal, Kieffer accepted to pay a "friendly" visit to Christian in his cell at the Cherche-Midi prison. Kieffer's appearance bore witness to the two weeks he had spent in prison.

However, without the slightest hint of suspicion, Christian readily revealed to his comrade, whom he knew well, the information so greatly coveted by Hugo Bleicher: Armand's address: 8 Villa Léandre, Montmartre. No-one was aware that, at that precise instant, Armand, together with a radio-operator, Maurice and the "Aviation" chief, Bourcier, alias Volta, were celebrating the network's first anniversary in the aforementioned villa. A message had even been sent from London, "Happy anniversary to the whole family".[73] On the same evening, as a reward for his collaboration, Kieffer spent the night alone with his mistress in a hotel in Boulevard de Grenelle.

On the following morning, by 05.30 hours, the quarter was totally surrounded. Villa Léandre, situated in Rue Junot, was ambushed in an immense commotion. Armand was arrested, together with his companion Renée Borni. However, the operation had been carelessly prepared and was not a complete success. The Abwehr had initially rung the doorbell of number 8bis, thus raising the alert. Thanks to this flagrant mistake, Maurice and Volta had been able to escape via one of the villa windows. The Cat was not in the villa. She had spent the night in her apartment at 6 Avenue Lamarck. She was, however, arrested a few hours later as she prepared to enter into Villa Léandre,

[73] Henri Noguères (under the auspices of), **Histoire de la Résistance en France, Part 2, Ju ly 1941-October 1942**, Robert Laffont, Paris, 1969, page 214.

the Germans having been crafty enough to leave... a mouse-trap.

Kieffer fully realised. He had directly contributed towards the decline of the Interallié network's chief. Sergeant Bleicher had just accomplished a master feat, and had no intention of stopping there. He would annihilate the entire network. With the willing contribution of the Cat who had immediately accepted to work for the Abwehr, following that of Lemeur who,

---

[74] *The consequences of the betrayal were considerable. Throughout November and December 1941, the Abwehr arrested some 70* **Interallié** *agents, according to the Ast-Saint-Germain chief,* **Oscar Reile**. *Detained in Fresnes prison,* **Roman Czerniawski**, *the network's chief was offered a quite unexpected proposal by Reile. To avoid the* **Interallié** *agents from facing the German court-martial, the Polish officer was asked to work secretly for the Germans from England. Reile made three attempts at convincing Czerniawski and the third proved to be successful. According to the German counter espionage agent, a written agreement was even signed between the two men in May 1942. All they needed to do was to simulate Czerniawski's escape during his transfer from the prison to the place where his interrogation was to take place, on the 14th of July, while the Capital's streets were crowded to celebrate Bastille Day. The false escape was, of course, a total success and Roman Czerniawski reached England where he immediately informed the secret services of the transformation of prisoners into hostages. In order to avoid their lives being put to risk, the British sent messages to the Abwehr, according to the code agreed between Roman and Reile, but whose contents were evidently of little danger to the Allies. Information continued to be provided for approximately two years, wrote Reile. However, he was convinced that such trivial information had not been sent by* **Armand**. *Despite his strong suspicion, Reile respected his side of the deal and none of the Resistance fighters arrested from the* **Interallié** *network faced a court-martial. Some of them were even released, however, contrary to Reile's account, many were sent to* **concentration camps** *in Germany where they perished in the most appalling conditions.*

in Cherbourg, had done the same, and then, thanks to his latest recruit, *Raoul*, he achieved his goal in the space of only five weeks.[74]

The train had just left Evreux station. Their tickets had been controlled without incident. Graham dozed, or pretended to do so. *Bob* smoked a cigarette in the corridor. How long had Kieffer known him? Only a few months. To be honest, he knew very little about him. His real name was Robert Goubeau. Just like Kieffer, he was a member of Interallié. Bleicher had had him arrested approximately a month after Kieffer; he was one of his latest recruits. He had hesitated less than Kieffer before accepting the enemy camp. Arrested on the 6th of December 1941 at the "Louis XIV" café, he had immediately accepted treason and was released a mere three days later. He was the man who informed Bleicher of the existence of the Overcloud network, run by the Le Tac brothers, and whose headquarters were in Rue Gît-le-Coeur in Paris. Kieffer remembered that rendezvous at the "Dupont Latin" café when, together with Goubeau, he had met one of the network members. In order to further penetrate the network, Bleicher had infiltrated the Cat, whom Goubeau had introduced as the perfect secretary and typist. The treason plan was prepared and organised between Goubeau and the Cat, under the orders of Bleicher, at 4 Rue Porto-Riche, Saint-Germain-en-Laye. They were to await the return of the Le Tac brothers, who were preparing a trip to England, before arresting them. But it was finally Kieffer and Goubeau who were to finalise the mission, under the supervision of Commander Ische and his men, Bleicher and the Cat having totally abandoned the affair at the end of December to concentrate on infiltrating the Autogiro network run by

[75] **Pierre de Vomécourt** *had reached England with the 7th* **Cameronians** *after the Battle of Dunkirk. He was one of the first French agents to join the* **SOE**. *Parachuted into Valençay, in the Indre region, on the night of the 10th of May 1941, he was soon to form the* **Autogiro** *network in the occupied zone, working under the pseudonym of* **Lucas**. *Deprived of radio contact with England, he made contact with* **Victoire**, *another of Mathilde Carré's pseudonyms, unaware of the fact that she had pledged alliance with the Abwehr. She was soon to be unmasked by de Vomécourt who managed to convert her yet again, and whilst tricking Bleicher into believing that she was still working for the Abwehr, he succeeded, with great difficulty, in taking her to England in a speed boat on the night of the 26th of February 1942. Parachuted once more within the occupied zone, on the night of the 1st of April 1942, Pierre de Vomécourt was arrested on the 25th of April, following the interception of one of his couriers at the demarcation line. Imprisoned at Fresnes prison, he was lucky to be given the status of war prisoner and spent 18 months in Oflag IV C until the Liberation.*

[76] *We invite readers to consult the moving book written by Monique Le Tac, and recounting the story of Joël and Yves Le Tac's mother, entitled* **Yvonne Le Tac, une femme dans le siècle (de Montmartre à Ravensbrück),** *Editions Tirésias, Paris, 2000, 156 pages. Joël Le Tac was only a few days from his 24th birthday when he was arrested on the 5th of February 1942 in Rennes. Imprisoned in Angers, then Fresnes, he was deported to Natzweiler-Struthof concentration camp, under the "N.N." category. He was then sent, after successive evacuations, to Dachau (POW number 103.196), Gross Rosen, Dora and finally Bergen-Belsen from where he was released. His brother Yves, 10 years his senior, was arrested in Paris on the 6th of February 1942, together with his companion, Andrée Conte. Initially imprisoned in Fresnes prison, just like his brother, he was deported to Natzweiler-Struthof under the "N.N." category, and, during the camp's evacuation on the 6th of September 1944, he was transferred to Dachau (POW n° 103.197). He was also fortunate enough to return home in 1945.*

Pierre de Vomécourt (Lucas).[75] The Le Tac brothers were arrested on the 5th and 6th of February 1942.[76]

Since then, Kieffer had been far from "idle". Together with his accomplice Goubeau, alias *Bob*, he had received orders to return to Brittany to inform Bleicher of the activities of a certain Melle Hélène de Plœuc[77], suspected of maintaining contacts with London. He was then sent to Marseille, again with *Bob*, but also with Jouffret[78], who had also converted to the Abwehr after his arrest, and who was destined to infiltrate another of the Resistance networks. And finally, there was the famous infiltration of Paul Hautechaud's network in the Pays d'Auge.

How had Bleicher come to learn of the existence of Resistance networks in Normandy? Following the arrest of Pierre de Vomécourt, in Paris on the 25th of April 1942, the non-commissioned officer from the Abwehr had learned that a certain Burdeyron, alias Cavali, from Caen was suspected of organising two sabotage operations on the Paris-Cherbroug railway line.[79] Bleicher had succeeded in arresting the Resistance fighter near to Saint-Lazare station in Paris on the 9th of May 1942. In order to avoid the firing

---

[77] *On the 1st of October 1942 **Hélène de Plœuc** was arrested and deported to Aix-la-Chapelle, Gelsenkirchen and Breslau, and then to the concentration camps of Ravensbrück, Mauthausen and Bergen-Belsen where she died in March-April 1945.*

[78] ***Claude Jouffret**, alias **Michel, Interallié** agent, was arrested on the 18th of November 1941. He was to be released after two months' detention at Fresnes prison, on the 22nd of January 1942.*

squad, Berdeyron had accepted to write three letters of recommendation concerning Kieffer. The first was sent to Jean Réveillard in Caen, the second to another Resistance fighter in Lisieux and the third to his wife. He told her that he had to go to London for a few weeks and that Kieffer was an agent from Paris in whom she could have the utmost confidence. It was hence that Kieffer and Jouffret were sent to Caen and Lisieux to infiltrate the Normandy Resistance.

Kieffer initially moved to Burdeyron's apartment in Caen[80] and became acquainted with a number of Resistance fighters in Caen. He then headed for Lisieux where he managed to establish links with Dr Hautechaud in Fervaques. The latter then introduced him to Roland Bloch[81] (alias Hugo), who ran the Lisieux sector. Bloch, in turn, introduced Kieffer to several of the town's network members and put him in contact with many Resistance fighters from Caen including "Ceux de la Résistance" (those from the Resistance), and in particular, the naval officer Pierre Comby[82] (alias Boileau) and Emmanuel

[79] **Bleicher** was ill-informed. The notorious attacks of the nights of the 15th and the 30th of April 1942 on the Paris-Cherbourg railway line, at Airan, had in fact been carried out by one of the Calvados FTP (Francs Tireurs et Partisans) teams. The sabotage is described in Jean Quellien's book, **Résistance et Sabotages en Normandie**, Editions Charles Corlet, Condé-sur-Noireau, 1992, republished in 2004.

[80] Captain **Noël Burdeyron** was parachuted close to Mortain (Orne) on the 9th of July 1941, in order to organise the SOE network in the Caen-Avranches region. His radio-operator, Lieutenant **Ernest Bernard**, was unfortunately arrested shortly afterwards by the French Police. Burdeyron was, himself, arrested on the 9th of May 1942 and imprisoned in Fresnes prison from where he was sent to a POW camp until April 1945.

Robineau[83] (alias Riquet) who was in charge of parachute drops and was to become the head of the BOA.

On his return from his "inspection missions" which took place two or three times a month, Kieffer who was occasionally accompanied by Jouffret, but more often by Goubeau, gave a detailed report of his many contacts to Bleicher. Hence, as from the spring of 1942, Dr Hautechaud's network was under the close surveillance of the Abwehr. Kieffer, whom Bleicher referred to as Kiki, had become the key protagonist of a network that the German counterespionage called: Lisiana, its hub being situated in Lisieux. Every single piece of information gleaned by the

---

[81] **Roland Bloch** was arrested on the 6th of October 1943 in Lisieux, with compromising documents in his possession. Imprisoned in Caen, he was later transferred to Bonne Nouvelle prison in Rouen and was condemned to death on the 10th of November by the **Feldkommandantur 517** Military Court in Rouen. He was executed on the 13th of November 1943, at the Madrillet firing range, Route d'Elbeuf, **Grand Quevilly**.

[82] **Pierre Comby**, staff member of **Ceux de la Résistance** (C.D.L.R.), camouflaged his Resistance activities behind the company name "Société des Tourbières de Normandie" (Normandy Peat Company), located in Place Saint-Sauveur in Caen, and which provided a letter box for the movement. Sure that he was under surveillance, he warned his group members, advising them to be particularly prudent. He consequently escaped the Gestapo raid on Caen in December 1943, which was to annihilate the best part of the Resistance movement in Calvados.

[83] Another C.D.L.R. member, in charge of the difficult task of dealing with arms, **Emmanuel Robineau**, was to become the local BOA chief **(Aerial Operations Bureau)** in the Calvados region, following the merger between the C.D.L.R and the O.C.M. **(Civil and Military Organisation)**. He was arrested by the SD (Security Service) in Caen on the 15th of December 1943 and was brutally tortured before being hastily shot down on the 1st of February 1944 during a pseudo escape attempt at Rougemoutiers (Eure region).

members of the Resistance: messages, documents of all sorts, reports, photographs, maps, plans all ended up, via *Raoul*, on Bleicher's desk. Bleicher had now become the great manipulator of a Resistance network and, henceforth, no important piece of information escaped his attention.

As soon as Kiki had spoken to Bleicher of the British officer, Graham Hayes, taken in by the Lisiana group mid-September, Bleicher had immediately exulted in such a godsend. Thanks to Hayes, he was perhaps on the verge of unmasking an escape network to Spain. He wanted to be there, at Saint-Lazare station, as soon as Hayes arrived.

Raoul and *Bob* were to hand Graham over to Bleicher on the railway platform. The train was due to arrive in only a few minutes. The most hurried travellers were already encumbering the corridor with their luggage. *Raoul* nodded to Graham to prepare himself to leave the train. The British officer still appeared calm. It was just as well. The express train was now travelling at slow speed and had just passed under the Pont de l'Europe. The three men stood up at the same time, put their raincoats on, retrieved their cases from the baggage rack and calmly joined the flock of travellers who tensely waited for the train to grind to a halt. *Bob* was still as sullen as when the train had left Lisieux. *Raoul* winked at Graham as if to say to him to pay no attention to their unpleasant companion. Raoul had in no time distinguished Bleicher who was waiting at the end of the platform with another man, despite the bustling crowd that rushed anxiously towards the exit. Railway station controls were always dreaded.

CHAPTER IV
GRAHAM'S DISAPPEARANCE

The encounter between the five men was only to last a few minutes. Rapid handshakes were exchanged. *Raoul* rapidly introduced Graham to Monsieur Paul.

"He organised everything", he said, pointing to Bleicher, "And this is Armand, he'll put you up for a few days".

When it was time for them to separate, with a vigorous handshake, Graham expressed his sincere gratitude to his two escorts, *Raoul* and *Bob*, before saying goodbye to Monsieur Paul. No-one lingered. It was hardly the place for effusiveness.

As he approached the station exit towards Cour du Havre, *Raoul* turned round one last time to see Graham disappear down the stairway leading to the metro accompanied by his newfound protector. Mission accomplished, he thought to himself, with certain unease as he noticed the joyful expression on Bleicher's face. *Raoul* had been promised a healthy bonus for this prized catch. Capturing a British officer was far from commonplace in German counterespionage.

An hour later, the two men reached their destination, 38 Avenue du Maréchal Foch in Garches (Seine-et-Oise region)[84], which was the home of Armand, whose true name was Jean-Louis Ortet.

Born in Bône (Algeria), Ortet had fought in the First World War, as a French Foreign Legion officer. Wounded and awarded with medals, he ended the war with the rank of Captain.

When peace reigned again, he became a sales representative for a German shoe manufacturer. He travelled a lot, but the war had transformed the ex-Legionnaire into another man. His head injuries were such that they had altered his mental capacity to such an extent that, in 1938, he committed a serious crime that was to bring him before the Criminal Court. His lawyer appealed to the jury by praising his excellent service in the Legion and his medals, and after having insisted on his diminished mental capacities rendering him unaccountable for his acts, Ortet was acquitted.

Over the following years, Ortet lived a dissolute life and frequented the most undesirable individuals. During the first years of the Occupation, he complemented his professional activity with black market

---

[84] **Garches** *is nowadays located in the French administrative department n° 92, the Hauts-de-Seine.*

trading. The Germans were perfectly aware of his somber legal history and readily left him to continue his fruitful business. By taking advantage of his weaknesses, and by exerting pressure and blackmail on him, they managed to extort a certain number of favours, thus transforming him into a counterespionage agent.

Hence, Ortet became one of the Abwehr's sub-agents, placed directly under the orders of Sergeant Bleicher, alias Monsieur Paul. In reality, he knew very little of the man he was to accommodate for around two weeks in his home in Garches. He had been told that he was a British officer and that he was to keep a close eye on him without arousing suspicion. When the time was right, he would be given instructions to take him to the Spanish border.

Graham felt immediately safe with this man who proved to be obliging and even considerate towards him. He decided to occupy the first days of the second phase of his escape by writing to his friends in Normandy. He had the time to inform them that all was well. *Raoul* had come back to see him the day after his move to Garches, and he had told Graham that he would personally deliver his letters to Normandy, since he liaised at least once a month between the Parisian headquarters and Dr Hautechaud's network.

On the same evening, Graham, who had easily obtained pen and paper from Armand, set to thanking Suzanne Septavaux for her warm welcome and for her dedication. In his letter, he added his best regards to Suzanne's nephew, Emmanuel Des Georges, and thanked her friend Septime Humann who had accompanied him from Bayeux to Le Pin. Without taking a break, he drafted a second letter, this time addressed to Dr Paul Hautechaud, and once more, expressing his sincere gratitude for the care that he had dispensed and for their long conversations that had been of precious value to Graham's morale.

Graham gave the letters to *Raoul* who, as soon as he returned to see Bleicher at their usual meeting place, 4 Rue Porto-Riche in Saint-Germain-en-Laye, handed them to the German for him to make copies. With these two letters, the Abwehr's non-commissioned officer held the material proof of the connivance with the enemy of the chief of the Jean-Marie network's Normandy section, and of three of its agents. He would put it to good use when he himself judged fit to do so. A few weeks later, *Raoul* delivered the two letters to their destination, hence striking the ultimate blow to his own betrayal.[85]

In Garches, Armand was at a loss as to how to entertain his guest who was becoming more and more impatient to rejoin England. In the neighbourhood, he knew an English woman whom he had contacted in 1940, before converting to enemy collaboration, to help him to work for the Intelligence Service.

On one of the last days of October 1942, Armand accompanied Graham to number 245 Grande Rue in

[85] After having handed Captain Hayes over to the Abwehr, **Robert Kieffer** continued to penetrate the Resistance networks, providing regular information to **Hugo Bleicher** on the Normandy group activities until the massive Gestapo arrests in Caen, around Lisieux and in the Pays d'Auge in September and October 1943. In November 1943, Kieffer facilitated the arrest of two young runaway Resistance fighters from Trouville, **Henri Dobert** and **René Capron**, who were to be executed by the firing squad the following month together with four other Resistance fighters from Calvados. He was also directly or indirectly (with the complicity of another traitor, **Robert Alesh**, appointed by the Abwehr and executed at the Liberation) accessory to the arrest and deportation of 19 other Resistance members of the sub-network Jean-Marie/Donkeyman (of whom eight died in Nazi concentration camps).

In the spring of 1944, he left to seek a second virginity in the underground Resistance forces in the Yonne region, just after another ex-double agent, **Roger Bardet**, the **Jean-Marie/Donkeyman** network's number two man. Bardet excelled by his bravery and his determination. Kieffer fully understood the lesson. On his return to Normandy around May 1944, he reunited the remaining Resistance groups of the Jean-Marie sub-network; those that had survived the arrests of autumn 1943, which had annihilated the quasi-totality of Dr Hautechaud's organisation. He managed to arm the groups via two parachute deliveries made by the SOE, one in Meulles on the 16th of May, the other in Bellou on the 25th of May 1944. Still using the same pseudonym of Raoul, but also known as **Michel de Normandie**, he endeavoured relentlessly to create liaisons between the several small groups of the FFI in the region of Lisieux, Broglie and Vimoutiers, who, since the 6th of June 1944, carried out efficient and incessant guerrilla activities behind the German lines (sabotage of telephone lines and railway tracks, destruction of rail bridges, laying of mines and tire puncturing devices on secondary roads, etc.). On the 18th of August 1944, he contacted the British Army and left for England at the end of the month, managing to obtain the ratification by the SOE of the totality of the FFI groups' activities in the Pays d'Auge, to his personal advantage.

After the Liberation, the French authorities were flooded with complaints from a number of survivors from the Jean-Marie/Donkeyman network and from the families of the executed, deported or missing members, and managed to have Kieffer extradited by Great Britain on the 1st of October 1944. He was handed over to military security, interrogated, then released, before finally being imprisoned at the Santé prison in Paris in December 1944. He was subsequently questioned by the D.G.E.R., and maintained in detention while awaiting his trial and that of his co-defendants: Roger Bardet, Robert Goubeau, Claude Jouffret and Marie-Suzanne Renouf. The trial was opened on the 5th of December 1949, before the **Seine Court of Justice in Paris**, with the reading of a particularly voluminous bill of indictment comprising some 177 pages. Kieffer, Bardet, Goubeau and Jouffret, **were charged with spying for the Abwehr**. Suzanne Renouf was also among the defendants for having been Bleicher's mistress. The **Bardet-Kieffer affair** immediately hit the headlines of the Parisian dailies (L'Aurore, Franc-Tireur, Le Monde) during the ten days hearing. The fourth day was devoted to one of the charges held against Kieffer: the arrest and the death of Captain Graham Hayes. Suzanne Septavaux and Emmanuel Des Georges were called to the bar as prosecution witnesses on the 8th of December. Suzanne Septavaux accused Kieffer of having deliberately handed the British officer over to the Germans, while her nephew judged him directly responsible, together with Bardet, for the death of his two comrades from Trouville.

On the **16th of December 1949**, the sentence was delivered after three and a half hours deliberation: **Bardet and Kieffer** were found guilty and were both **sentenced to death**, to national degradation and to the confiscation of their personal assets. Goubeau was sentenced to 5 years forced labour and national degradation. Jouffret was to serve 4 years imprisonment, to pay a 12,000 Franc fine and to suffer national degradation. And finally, Suzanne Renouf was sentenced to 3 years imprisonment, a fine of 100,000 Francs, national degradation and the confiscation of her personal assets.

Kieffer and Bardet, who had received the death sentence, were, in fact, released, after having benefited from the amnesty law of the 6th of August 1953. Robert Kieffer died on the 22nd of September 1974 in Senlis (Oise).

Garches. Mrs Davidson immediately recognised the man she had met two years previously and that she had occasionally bumped into in the street.

As soon as they had been introduced, Graham took an immediate liking to the young mother of two, whose husband had been arrested by the Germans as a national of one of the countries at war with the Reich. Mrs Davidson had, herself, been arrested on the same grounds, together with her husband and their two children, however, due to their young age, she and the children had been released. Her husband had been detained for a while, with many of his compatriots who had been arrested throughout France, in a barracks in Saint-Denis before being transferred to the Vittel civil internment camp (Vosges region).

Graham spoke to Mrs Winifred C. Davidson in English, and it was a great joy for him to finally express himself freely and fluently in his mother tongue. On the first day, they only stayed an hour. No need to take advantage of her kindness or to cause her any unpleasant neighbourhood gossip. Graham had, however, had the time to recount his raid across the Channel and to tell her of his ten comrades in arms, and in particular of Major March-Phillips. He explained the defeat of their mission, their unfortunate encounter with a German patrol alerted by a guard dog, the impossibility of regaining the speed boat, the machine gunfire and the explosion that had thrown them all overboard, his desperate attempt to save his commander before abandoning him, inanimate in the cold Channel waters. He then explained how he reached the beach, shattered, without being located, and how he was taken in by the Normandy Resistance and led to Garches, whilst awaiting an escape route via Spain.

Mrs Davidson appeared to be deeply moved by Graham's account. She wondered how she could help this young man, handsome and so typically British, and who still bore a scar on the left of his chin. She invited him to pay her visits whenever he wished, whilst awaiting his departure for Spain. Graham was delighted to be able to confide in her and immediately accepted. They planned a second visit on the following afternoon.

During his second visit, Graham's discourse became more and more intense and earnest and, throughout the hours, Mrs Davidson became a genuine confidante and friend. He told her of his dear parents who were undoubtedly going through the most atrocious anxiety concerning his disappearance, and he gave her their address, Kiln Hill, Linton-on-Wharfe, Yorkshire. Perhaps she could somehow get a letter to them to reassure them before his return to England? Graham also asked her to write a brief message which he dictated to her, and to post it to Miss Jane Dreyer, in Cape Town, South Africa, "All well here. Do not worry. Graham sends his love also". On the following day, the 27th of October, the letter was posted by Mrs Davidson via the Red Cross.[85]

Graham knew that Jane Dreyer would manage to send the message to his parents. He still loved the young woman although they were not quite officially engaged. They had met at the end of 1941, during preparations for his first SOE mission in Africa: operation Postmaster. She was, at the time, attached to the FANY (First Aid Nursing Yeomanry), which also provided a cover for the female members of the SOE. Jane Dreyer was in fact secretary to the chief of the SOE mission in Cape Town.

From that day on, Graham paid regular visits to Mrs Davidson with whom he took great pleasure in discussing a variety of topics: his family of course, his friends, life in England during the Blitz, his after-war plans, and many other subjects. The two week wait had finally flown by. Then one day, Ortet informed Graham that he would be leaving two days later. Once more, it was time for farewells. Mrs Davidson had great difficulty in containing her emotion. What did the future hold? Would they see each other again? Graham had promised to let her know, one way or another, as soon as he reached England. He also gave his word

[85] *The letter reached its destination, but only on the 3rd of June 1943, after having been retained by postal censorship. Miss Dreyer immediately sent a telegram to Graham's mother: **"Have received glorious news from friends through Red Cross dated last October that Graham was well and sends love. Advise discretion writing"**. On the 11th of June, the Cape Town mission informed the SOE staff of the contents of this letter announcing that Graham Hayes was still alive at the date of the 27th of October 1942.*

that he would deliver, by hand, the letter that she had given him for her father who still lived in England.

When the day came, Ortet drove Graham to Paris and provided him with false identity papers. Ortet himself would escort Graham as far as the Pyrenean Mountains and the Spanish border. It was a hazardous trip. Controls were commonplace in railway stations. They would then have to cross the demarcation line, where identity papers were subject to severe scrutiny. At the last minute, Graham learned that three other soldiers would be travelling with them: two Australians and a Canadian. The five men boarded the express train to Toulouse at Austerlitz station in Paris. The crossing of the demarcation line was finally without incident, much to the relief of all. Ortet had everyone alight from the train, giving the excuse that he had important information to collect from the Resistance and that Graham was to take back to England.

From that point on, the archives are insufficient to reconstitute the end of the British Captain's journey. Upon his return to Garches, Ortet informed Mrs Davidson that all had gone well and that Captain Hayes had effortlessly crossed the Spanish border. They had alighted in a small village close to the frontier and a French guide, then a Spanish border escort had assisted them in reaching Spain.

The precise circumstances of Graham's arrest remain a mystery. It would appear that he was, indeed, arrested on Spanish territory, then handed over to the Germans at the border, a few days before the invasion of the south zone, on the 11th of November 1942. There is no doubt that the Germans were waiting for him. The Abwehr in Saint-Germain-en-Laye had informed their colleagues on the Spanish soil. Their agents had kept a close eye on the border for a long time, and the crossing of several German civilians had not escaped the surveillance of the French Vichy intelligence service throughout the duration of the free zone. The Germans were perfectly familiar with the route taken by Ortet, and all they needed to do was to prepare a trap at the other side of the border with the complicity of the local Spanish authorities. They had a precise description, as well as a photograph of Captain Hayes, which had been used to prepare his false identity papers. *Raoul* had looked after having the photograph copied by Bleicher's counterespionage service.

Graham was brought back to Paris by the Germans and imprisoned at Fresnes prison in the south of Paris. During interrogation, Bleicher revealed his true identity, telling Graham that he knew every last detail of his journey from his landing in Normandy to his arrival in Garches. He knew every single Resistance fighter that had helped him and he quoted their names: Dr Hautechaud[86], Suzanne Septavaux[87], Emmanuel Des Georges[88], Septime Humann[89]. It was a cruel blow to Graham who felt immense grief, not for himself but for his friends in Normandy. He could do nothing to help them. And to add insult to injury, he had severely jeopardised their safety by writing to them. Bleicher showed him copies of the letters written in Garches. *Raoul*'s treachery now appeared to him to be so blatantly evident.

Feelings of disgust mingled with revolt. What could he do?

[86] **Paul Hautechaud** was denounced and arrested on the 18th of September 1943, after having helped a Canadian bomber whose plane had crashed the previous day in the vicinity of Notre-Dame-de-Courson. The regional chief of the **Jean-Marie/Donkeyman** network was tortured by the Sipo-SD (Security Police) in Caen before being deported to Buchenwald concentration camp (POW n° 44 862), where he died of illness and exhaustion on the 11th of March 1944.

[87] **Suzanne Septavaux** was arrested on the 27th of April 1943, for having assisted Graham Hayes, and was imprisoned in Fresnes prison until the 20th of August 1943 when she was released.

[88] **Emmanuel Des Georges** escaped from arrest by going into hiding in the Yonne region where he fought, arms in hand, for one of the SOE's underground forces, under the orders of Commander Adam. After the D-Day landings in Normandy, he returned to Lisieux and participated in the Liberation combat as a member of the FFI (French Forces of the Interior).

[89] **Septime Humann** was arrested at Juaye-Mondaye on the 1st of May 1943, for the help given to Captain Hayes. Imprisoned in Fresnes prison, he was lucky to have a certain Bouchez as one of his fellow inmates. Bouchez' wife was German and was related to the General in command in Paris. As soon as Bouchez was released, he asked his wife to intervene in order to obtain the release of Septime Humann and Suzanne Septavaux who both left the prison on the 20th of August 1943.

In his prison cell, Graham had been put into solitary confinement. He mentally retraced the events since his arrest, his interrogation by Monsieur Paul, the Abwehr agent. Amidst this great disaster, however, he retained two feelings of relative content. Firstly, the German had promised that he would be sent to a POW camp. But should he trust him? Secondly, during the interrogation, Mrs Davidson's name had not been mentioned. Ortet had, therefore, held back certain information. Why?[90]

Just like the other prisoners at Fresnes, Graham Hayes rapidly grasped the Morse code communication system that had been established between neighbouring cells by knocking on the piping. The weeks went by. Graham was still in prison at Christmas and the New Year of 1943. When spring came, Graham was already one of the "oldest" of the prison's inmates. Many of his co-detainees had left for the firing squad, at Mont Valérien, or had been deported to Nazi concentration camps. Why had he not been transferred

---

[90] *Throughout the whole affair, **Ortet** remains an enigmatic character. He would appear to have played a double role: he was involved in several black market trading networks (he was even said to have been implicated in gold trading), had participated in Abwehr missions to infiltrate Resistance networks but had also worked for British Intelligence via Mrs Davidson. After Graham's arrest, he continued his mystifying role, making several trips to the Landes region for the SOE. He was found assassinated, in a pond in Bugé (Indre region) on the 1st of September 1943. Was it a case of vengeance between black market dealers or the discovery, either by the Abwehr or by the Resistance, of his dual activity?*

to a POW camp? Bleicher had evidently lied to him. Bleicher was no longer interested in his prisoner, and Graham remained at Fresnes as one of the Wehrmacht's "hostages".

Then summer came. Graham tapped on the pipes of his prison cell, but he did not receive the usual response. He concluded that there was a new inmate in the neighbouring cell. Hence, Graham established contact with a young English RAF officer who had been shot down from the French skies in June 1943. Their communication remained limited, but this new contact proved to be an excellent boost to Graham's morale. Each morning, he would cry "*Good morning*" to his invisible neighbour, Lieutenant J.E.C. Evans, who returned the compliment. When the sentry rounds were out of earshot, they would exchange information in Morse. The Air Force officer consequently learned that Graham had been in Fresnes prison for 8 months. He told him of his arrest in Spain, and that the Spaniards had handed him over to the Germans, before his transfer to Fresnes prison. Another day, Graham told Evans that they had promised to send him to a POW camp in Germany, but that he had started to wonder whether that would ever happen. In the evening, before going to sleep, they would both shout, "*Goodnight!*" Evans, who survived the war, recounted the great moral support that Graham offered him over the few weeks during which they maintained contact, with varying degrees of difficulty, from one cell to the next.

Then one evening, when Evans cried his customary, "*Goodnight*!", there was no response from Graham's cell, neither a shout nor a tap on the pipe. What could have happened to him?

On the afternoon of that same day, whose date is difficult to trace; was it a few days before his execution, or the very day; the German sentry came to collect Graham in his cell. At that precise moment in time, Graham was oblivious to where they were taking him, or why he was to leave the prison. The German had not pronounced those terrifying words that were such a source of anguish among detainees, but that allowed, nevertheless, a glimmer of hope: "Interrogation", "Court" or "Transport".

Where was Graham Hayes executed?

Whereas all sources tend to agree on the date of his execution, they appear to be contradictory as to the precise location. According to unnamed "official French sources", Graham Hayes was shot down on the 13th of July 1943 at 4.03 pm in the 15th arrondissement in Paris. The precise location is not mentioned. According to other information gathered after the war by Graham's parents from the British military authorities, the British officer is said to have been executed at the Fort of Mont Valérien in Suresnes, on the outskirts of Paris. One thing is certain; he was buried in the Parisian cemetery at Ivry where he was found after the Liberation by an SOE member.[91]

Why did the Germans execute him?

At the end of the war, a document found in the German archives at Potsdam, and discovered by the British army while enquiring on war crimes, maintains the mystery surrounding Graham Hayes' death. In a few lines, the document reads:

"Landing operation at Port-en-Bessin".

The death sentence was pronounced against Captain Graham Hayes, born on the 9th of July 1914 in Leeds. Hayes landed close to Cherbourg with a relatively large group of commandos on the 13th of September 1942. As he retreated, his boat was destroyed. He swam back to the beach and remained in hiding for a month in civilian clothing among the French, engaging in spying activities, collecting information on possible landing zones and looking to recruit agents. He was followed by one of our agents and was unmasked. He was arrested in Paris on the 28th of October 1942. On the 22nd of February 1943, he was condemned to death by the Commanding Court in Paris. The sentence was executed on the 13th of July 1943".[92]

---

[91] *Graham Hayes' remains were transferred from the Parisian cemetery of Ivry to the town cemetery in **Viroflay**, on the 1st of May 1951, following a decision by the **Commonwealth War Graves Commission**. One can, however, still visit his first grave which remains intact in Ivry cemetery.*

CAPTAIN
G. HAYES. M.C.
THE BORDER REGIMENT
COMMANDO
13TH JULY 1943 AGE 29

FAITHFUL EVEN UNTO DEATH.
HE GAVE HIS LIFE.
THAT WE MIGHT LIVE.
YET DID NOT DIE.

The first of Graham Hayes' graves in Ivry cemetery, 44 Avenue de Verdun, 94200 Ivry. The grave is situated in the small cemetery, 39th division, line 3, sepulchre 71. The grave is maintained by the association "Souvenir Français". There is an error in the text on the gravestone, Graham being spelled "Gream". "HAYES Gream Mort pour la France le 13-7-1943" (HAYES Gream Who died for France 13-7-1943).

Photograph of Graham Hayes' second grave in Viroflay town cemetery.

HAYES GREAM
MORT POUR LA FRANCE le   13-7-1943

Whereas the first part of the document is accurate, the second, apart from the execution date, is evidently a tissue of lies. The spying accusations are clearly pure fantasy. The date and place of arrest are false. The time span between the death sentence pronounced by a poorly identified court in Paris and the execution, five months later, appears to be highly unlikely. Graham never appeared before a German court. He would surely have informed his neighbouring cellmate, Evans, if such had been the case. However, after the war, the latter reported to Graham's parents their son's high spirits and his expectation to be sent to a German POW camp.

The Germans clearly wanted his death. They needed to execute hostages in an attempt to terrorise the population thus discouraging them from joining or supporting the Resistance. They needed to justify their acts and find a legal "disguise" for this war crime. Accusing Graham of spying was convenient. It was an accusation frequently used by the German courts and that enabled them to send thousands of French patriots and foreigners to the firing squad or to concentration camps.

---

[92] *This document is part of a file of several papers which were conserved, in 1945, in the **Cour de Potsdam archives**, "Division 463, Potsdam am Kanal 68, Geschg. St. LV 89/43 ", translated into English and now filed among the British National Archives of the **Public Record Office** under the code: DEFE 2/365. We were, unfortunately, unable to find the other documents belonging to the same file.*

Part four:

THE AQUATINT MEMOIRS

CHAPTER I
WHAT BECAME OF AQUATINT'S SURVIVORS?

Eight of the eleven men who landed on the beach at Saint-Laurent-sur-Mer, on the night of the 12th of September, were taken prisoner by the Germans. We can recall that four of them were captured on the beach the very day of the commando raid; Boatswain André Desgrange, Lieutenant Tony Hall, Captain Francis Howard and Sergeant Tom Winter.

Three others, Captain John Burton, and Privates Abraham Opoczynski (Adam Orr) and Jan Hellings who had attempted to flee, inopportunely came face to face with a German parachute unit only four days after the raid. All of them, with the exception of Tony Hall and Lord Howard, both wounded, were taken to Rennes, then dispatched to POW camps in Germany.

And finally, Captain Graham Hayes, taken in by the Resistance, managed to leave France for Spain, however, betrayed, he was eventually tracked down and handed over to the Germans who, after having detained him for several months in Fresnes prison, executed him in circumstances that remain, to this day, mysterious.

So what became of the seven other prisoners?

Lord Howard was the first of the commando's survivors to make his way back home. He was initially sent to a hospital in Germany where a POW regime was employed. Just like the other wounded or sick, he was deprived of his liberty, however, he was provided with a few simple material benefits. Hence, he obtained the necessary paper and coloured pencils to draw caricatures of himself, of his compatriots and of some of the German doctors and officers. He was granted sanitary repatriation to England, via Sweden, in 1943 and was admitted to Nuffield Hospital in Oxford, where Professor Trueta, an eminent Catalan surgeon who had fled the Frankish regime, managed to save his foot despite the onset of gangrene.

On the 1st of July 1944, he married Anne Bazley and the couple settled in his house at Dean Farm on the outskirts of Hatherop Estate in Gloucestershire. After the war, Lord Howard, whose war wounds had proved to be a genuine handicap, devoted himself essentially to his family, his farm and to local causes. He was designated chairman of the Bench and deputy Lord Lieutenant of Gloucestershire, before being appointed, in the 1950's, to a government land commission.

Lord Howard never forgot what had happened on that Normandy beach of Saint-Laurent-sur-Mer. He returned there with his wife in September 1986 and took the time to contemplate the graves of his three comrades buried in the small Calvados village cemetery. Lord Francis Howard of Penrith died on the 13th of November 1999, leaving behind his wife, four sons and a daughter-in-law that he considered as his own daughter.

Tony Hall returned to England after the German capitulation on the 8th of May 1945. Just like Francis, Howard, he remained disabled throughout his life following head and leg injuries received on the beach of Saint-Laurent-sur-Mer. He was operated on in Radcliffe Hospital in Oxford by a renowned surgeon, Professor Cairns who removed the grenade shrapnel from his leg. However, his prosthesis prevented him from driving and he suffered from regular fainting and epileptic fits. After the war, the BBC's Variety Department had kept his job open; however his state of health prevented him from resuming his professional activity. He therefore converted to antique dealing and became a genuine expert in the field, regularly consulted for advice from his very famous antique and objet d'art store in Clifton, one of Bristol's most exclusive districts.

Lord Francis HOWARD OF PENRITH

Portrait of Lord Francis of Penrith in the study of his home at Dean Farm, undated. (Private collection)

Lord Francis Howard, ▶
During his convalescence with Lady Anne Howard, No place, no date. (Private collection)

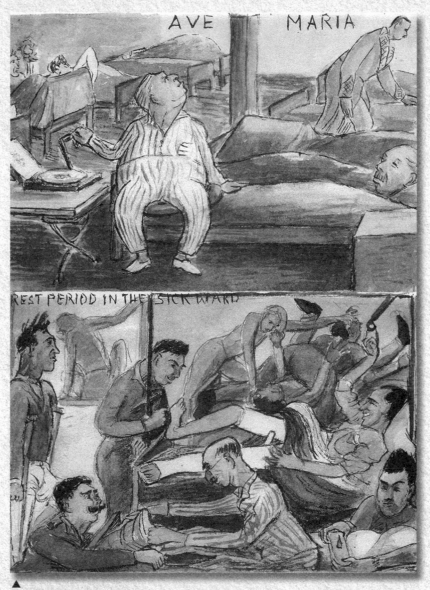

Two sketches by Lord Francis Howard during his convalescence in a German hospital. He represented himself on both drawings, on the left with his hair standing on end, bedridden in the top drawing and on crutches on the lower drawing. Late 1942. *(Private collection)*

Following an unexpected visit from Henrietta March-Phillips, the SSRF commander's daughter, he used his old radio contacts to obtain the broadcast of her father's story on the airwaves. A script involving several voices was written and the radio programme was recorded, then broadcast on the BBC airwaves on the 20th of August 1971. Tony Hall lived with Jane, the daughter of a wealthy labour peer, whom he met while she was working for an architect. Up to his death, Tony Hall nurtured fond memories of his pre-war trip to France, together with an immense respect and profound admiration for the French culture. André Heintz was moved when he received a letter from him, dated the 30th of January 1986, throughout which his taste for life, his cheerfulness, his sense of humour and his admirable courage still transpired.

Just like Tony Hall, John Burton spent the rest of the war in an officers' prison camp in Germany. After his liberation in 1945, the army sent him to Siam, and then to Sumatra at the very same time as the Japanese surrender. Upon his return to England in 1946, he met Anne, who was to become his wife the following year and the mother of one daughter. John Burton retired to South Africa where he died from cancer in 1985.

After a long and painful train trip, since the Germans had handcuffed him to avoid any attempt to escape, Tom Winter finally reached Stalag VIIIB in Larmsdorf, in Poland.[93] After a few weeks in captivity, he managed to find himself a job in the camp's postal service, thus maintaining contact with the British MI 9[94] via coded messages sent to his wife. He was also granted total freedom to circulate throughout the Stalag, and even to leave the camp, on the pretext of delivering parcels to the Red Cross. By doing so, he managed to perpetrate a few sabotage missions and even to liaise with members of the Polish Resistance, whom he taught to manipulate arms and explosives. When his clandestine activities were discovered, he was interned until such times as the Red Army advances forced the evacuation of prisoners to the West. He was then escorted, together with many of his co-detainees, to Stalag XI B in Fallingbostel, in the vicinity of Soltau and not far from Bergen-Belsen concentration camp.

Just before the British Army arrived at the camp, Winter managed to escape with another officer and to cross the lines until he reached the liberating army. Without wasting a second, he offered to serve as a

---

[93] **Lamsdorf** is now the Polish town of **Lambinowice.**

[94] **MI 9** stands for **Military Intelligence 9.** This British secret service was, as from 1940, in charge of organising European escape networks to facilitate the repatriation of military aircraft crews from planes shot down in enemy territory and of POW camp escapees.

guide to a British unit, thus providing assistance to his comrades still in captivity.

After the war, Tom Winter was only to return to France once, to walk once more on the Normandy soil and to pay homage to his comrades who had fallen on the beach of Saint-Laurent-sur-Mer. It was at the beginning of September 1994. The 90-year old ex-commando, was, at the time, the last remaining survivor of operation Aquatint. He died in 1996, in his home on the Isle of Wight, after having received several military honours and medals.

▲
The ex-commando Tom Winter (to the right of M Martin with his tricolour scarf) and Leslie Wright contemplates the graves of their comrades in the cemetery of Saint-Laurent-sur-Mer on the 11th of September 1994. (Chedal-Anglay collection)

The fate of Abraham Opoczynski remains somewhat unknown. He was separated from Tom Winter in the train that led him to Germany, quite precisely at Frankfurt-on-Main, according to Winter's account. The Gestapo indisputably had doubts as to his genuine identity. All trace of him was then lost. No-one ever saw him alive again. In 1986, the author and historian, Mike Langley was preparing a book on Anders Lassen, one of the members of the SSRF. He came across Abraham Opoczynski's grave in Durnbach cemetery in Bavaria, during his research on operation Aquatint, which he mentions in one of the chapters of his book, published in 1988. Further research via the website of the Commonwealth War Graves Commission, the official British body responsible for maintaining military graves abroad, confirmed this discovery, which in fact poses more questions than it provides answers. Abraham Opoczynski, is quoted as having died on Thursday 12th of April 1945 at the age of 23. His body was, indeed, buried in the military cemetery in Durnbach, a small Bavarian village, 10 miles from Bad Tölz, a town situated 30 miles from Munich. The cemetery holds some 2,933 graves of Commonwealth citizens, buried during the Second World War, most of them belonging to the Air Force and whose planes were bombed down by the Flak or during combat over Bavaria, Bade-Wurtemberg, Hesse, Thuringe or Austria. In the same cemetery, there are 29 non-British graves, almost all of them belonging to soldiers of Polish origin. In order to explain the presence of Abraham Opoczynski, we can only but formulate a hypothesis.

After "intensive" interrogation by the Gestapo, who knew only too well how to go about questioning, using methods that we are now familiar with, the true identity of Abraham Opoczynski, captured under the name of Adam Orr, had been discovered. He was then taken to Munich and to the nearby Dachau concentration camp. In other words, this prisoner of war, the Polish soldier Abraham Opoczynski, had become a "racial detainee", according to the name given by the Germans in concentration camps. Our second hypothesis is that he was then transferred to the Bad Tölz Kommando, where he was employed in an SS factory called the "S.S. Junkerschule". Perhaps it was within this Kommando that the operation Aquatint soldier died, thus explaining the presence of his grave in the German cemetery of Durnbach.

His companion, Jan Hellings' story is no clearer to us. We know, again thanks to Tom Winter's account, that the Dutchman was also questioned in Frankfurt by the Gestapo. In a letter sent to André Heintz on the 23rd of January 1986, Tom Winter talks of Hellings in the following terms,

"I was taken to Stalag 8B, shackled, and put in a compound with other commandos having the same treatment. Some months later I did meet up with Hellings, in another camp".

After being questioned by the Gestapo, Jan Hellings was therefore sent to a first Stalag, then transferred to a second, Stalag XI B, in Fallingbostel, where he met with Tom Winter. Did he survive up to the Liberation? He very probably did, otherwise the Commonwealth War Graves Commission would have found his grave in a British cemetery in Germany. So, what became of him after the war? Did he return to Holland? Alas, no-one has been able to enlighten us.

The French Naval officer, André Desgrange was sent to an Oflag and is said to have escaped and to have managed to reach England to continue his fight against Nazism. After the war, in December 1948, he remarried with Simone May in Paris, and put an end to his military career in 1951. He then settled in Angers (Maine-et-Loire) with his wife and their daughter, Claudette, where he occupied a management position in the regional hospital until his retirement in 1975.

He was awarded several French military distinctions (Officer of the Légion d'Honneur with rosette, Croix de Guerre with palm, Médaille de la Résistance, Croix du Combattant de la France Libre, Croix de la Libération) and British military distinctions (including the Conspicuous Gallantry Medal). He retired to Montbéliard (Doubs region), together with his wife, where he returned to his family roots. He died, in the same town, on the 7th of January 1990, and was laid to rest in Baume-les-Dames cemetery.

After a period of despondency, nurturing the hope that his comrades had somehow managed to escape, even those who had fallen into the hands of the Germans, Geoffrey Appleyard rapidly resumed combat within the SSRF. He took part in several new commando raids in the Channel Islands (in particular operation Basalt[95] on the Island of Sark on the night of the 3rd of October 1942).

After the disbanding of the SSRF, he was promoted to the rank of commander (Major), and received the Distinguished Service Order (DSO), "in recognition of gallant and distinguished services in the field", during a ceremony in Buckingham Palace at the beginning of February 1943. He was then, upon his own request, drafted to the 2nd SAS Regiment (Special Air Service), one of the RAF's commandos, and sent to North Africa.

---

[95] *Since the disappearance of Major March-Phillips, for whom he was second in command, Geoffrey Appleyard was named head of the SSRF, and he was the commander of operation **Basalt** on the **Island of Sark**. He was assisted by Captain Phillip Pinckney. The commando comprised 11 men of whom four originated from the N°12 Commando. The main aim of the raid was, as usual, to collect as much **information as possible on the enemy defence systems**, to bring back **prisoners** and to inflict as much damage as possible upon the enemy. There was a second objective to this particular raid; to bring back a Polish SOE agent, who had escaped from France and who had managed to reach the island with labourers from the Todt Organisation. The small group of commandos managed, without difficulty, to climb the 30 foot cliff leading to the Island of Sark. They reached a house in the hamlet of "La Jaspellière" where the owner, **Françoise Pittard**, an SOE agent, informed them that twenty or so German soldiers were accommodated at the Hôtel Dixart approximately 250 yards from her house. She informed them of a further five Germans in one of the hotel's annexes. Appleyard, who had decided to attack the smaller group,*

neutralised the sentries, before taking over the annexe and capturing the five Germans who were all asleep.

However, on their way back to the coast, the prisoners, who all had their hands tied behind their backs to facilitate their transport back to the "Doris", realising that they were being taken to a boat, attempted to alert their comrades at the hotel. One of them shouted back but was immediately shot down. The sound of gunfire immediately raised the alert. The Germans, now all outside the hotel, opened fire on the British commando. A second prisoner was stabbed by Anders Lassen in an attempt to escape and two others were also killed amidst the confusion. The group did however manage to re-embark with only one of the initial five prisoners, whilst the Germans continued firing at them. During the operation the polish officer, **Roman Zawadski**, was recovered with success by Captain Dudgeon and the commando's eleven men, together with their two passengers, finally boarded the MTB 344 safe and sound.

Operation **Basalt** was therefore a **partial success**. The SOE agent was repatriated, as planned, and the German non-commissioned officer consented to providing substantial information on the Channel Island defence systems, on military staffing and garrisons, on ongoing fortification works and on weapons. Concerning Sark, part of this information complemented that provided by Mme Pittard and by Roman Zawadski. However, the hasty retreat, and in particular the execution of four German soldiers found dead, their hands tied behind their backs, was to serve the Nazi cause and justify retaliation on captured allied commando members: systematic handcuffing, ill-treatment, up to heedless execution. Hitler's **directive n° 003830/42G**, signed on the 18th of October 1942, classified as "Top Secret" and addressed to all of the commanders of the Reich's units, declared, **"From now on all men operating against German troops in so-called Commando raids in Europe or in Africa, are to be annihilated to the last man. This is to be carried out whether they be soldiers in uniform, or saboteurs, with or without arms; and whether fighting or seeking to escape; and it is equally immaterial whether they come into action from Ships and Aircraft, or whether they land by parachute. Even if these individuals on discovery make obvious their intention of giving them-selves up as prisoners, no pardon is on any account to be given (...°)".**

Perhaps Graham Hayes, who had been handed over to the German SD after circulation of this directive, was purely and simply executed in accordance with the Führer's criminal decision.

During the conquest of Sicily, which began in July 1943, Geoffrey was among the first assault troops of the 1st Airborne Division, which had received orders to capture, by night, the bridge over Anapo River and the coastal batteries between Cassabile and Syracuse. Despite numerous military personnel and important naval and aerial resources, the American General Patton's bridgehead, to the South of the island, proved difficult to set up. The junction with units from the British Eighth Army, commanded by General Montgomery and who had landed further east, only took place on the 12th of July, after Patton's decision to drop 2,000 paratroopers during the night. German aviation remained particularly active. A cargo loaded with ammunition was even sunk in the Port of Gela. The whole affair made the allied DCA gunners very nervous. In such circumstances, it would appear that the plane transporting Geoffrey Appleyard was accidentally shot down on the night of the 12th to the 13th of July 1943. A disturbing coincidence, that Geoffrey Appleyard should lose his life on the 13th of July 1943, the very same day as his childhood friend, Graham Hayes, who, a few hours later, faced a German firing squad in Paris.

CHAPTER II
IS THERE A BRITISH REMEMBRANCE OF AQUATINT?

For the British, the SSRF raid, carried out on the 13th of September 1942 on the Calvados coast to the west of Port-en-Bessin was an out-and-out failure. Following a navigation error, the commando landed at Saint-Laurent-sur-Mer, instead of Sainte-Honorine-des-Pertes - the commando's target, and operation Aquatint rapidly turned into a complete fiasco. The eleven men commanded by Major March-Phillips, were unfortunate to come face to face with a German patrol which immediately alerted the entire zone. All of the commandos, as we have already mentioned, were either killed or taken prisoner. The commander of the MTB speedboat, together with its crew, including Captain Appleyard who acted as navigator, were the only commando members who managed to return to England safe and sound.

It is of surprise to no-one, neither in the British Army, nor in any other army in the world, that it is not customary to commemorate defeats, but victories. In the Secret War section, on the first floor of the Imperial War Museum in London, there is a large area devoted to the SOE's activities where visitors can read, via an interactive video terminal, a page summing up the brilliant success of operation Postmaster, on the Spanish island of Fernando Po in Spanish Guinea on the night of the 14th of January 1942. Our readers will, of course, remember the importance of this mission in the creation of the Small Scale Raiding Force.

To our knowledge, in the United Kingdom, there is no memorial, not even the humblest of plaques to commemorate the raid on the Normandy coast. So, one cannot honestly talk of the collective British remembrance of operation Aquatint. However, the memory of some of its protagonists has not been completely forgotten.

Two of the SSRF's men, Graham Hayes and Geoffrey Appleyard, both from the same English region of Yorkshire and whose parents lived in the same village of Linton-on-Wharfe, near Wetherby, together with five other young men from the same village, lost or fallen during military service[96], were, and still are today, the source of a genuine remembrance cult.

---

[96] Lieutenant A.R. Cooke, Captain **Malcolm Hayes (Graham's brother)**, Flight-Sergeants R.H. Heydon, Sidney Hilder and William Hilder (brothers).

The local press, expressed its emotion concerning the disappearance of Graham Hayes and of his brother Malcom[97], a 23-year old RAF Lieutenant, for the first time in an article published in the **Evening Post** on the 22nd of February 1943, and repeated, together with their photographs, in the **Yorks Evening Post** on the 23rd of February. The same newspaper announced, in its 7th of September issue, the disappearance of Geoffrey Appleyard during an operation in Sicily, after the War Office had informed his parents of the terrible news.

As soon as the war was over, Mr and Mrs Hayes, who complained of the slowness of the British Army's attempts to obtain information on Graham, engaged in personal research, parallel to that carried out by the SOE officer, Captain Planel.

[97] **Malcolm Cedric Hayes** was a Lieutenant in the 295th Squadron of the **Royal Air Force Volunteer Reserve**. He died, when his aircraft fell on Friday the 19th of February 1943. Malcolm Hayes was aboard one of the five Halifax bombers whose target was the electric transforming station in Coudray-Macouard/Distré, in the district of Montreuil-Bellay, a borough of Saumur. According to René G. Marnot's book, **Ma ville sous la botte**, Edition Roland, Paris, Lieutenant Hayes' Halifax was flying too low and hit a high voltage cable, exploding in flight close to the electric transforming station. The bomber's eleven crew members were immediately killed and their bodies remained, for several days, stretched across the vineyards amidst the debris of their aircraft. Every day, crowds would come from Saumur and its surroundings to pay homage to their remains, until their action stirred the Germans into having them buried in **Saumur town cemetery** on the 22nd of February. On the day of their burial, the cemetery was out of bounds to any civilians, however on the days that were to follow, the author wrote, there was an "unceasing procession of inhabitants from Saumur who came to scatter flowers on the graves of the eleven aviators".

The latter went to France at the end of September 1944 to find Mrs Winifred Davidson who had, for several weeks, received visits from Graham Hayes in Garches, when he was, as she believed, under the protection of the Resistance whilst awaiting an escape network via Spain. After Graham's departure, she had sent a message via the Red Cross to Jane Dreyer, an SOE agent in Cape Town, on the 27th of October 1942, announcing that Graham was well. The message only reached its destination on the 3rd of June 1943; however it was immediately transferred by telegram to Graham's parents, and confirmed to the SOE by the Cape Town mission on the 11th of June.

Mrs Winifred Davidson encouraged the enquiring officer to track down Ortet, the man with whom Captain Hayes had been accommodated during his stay in Garches, however Ortet had also disappeared. During the summer of 1945, the enquiry went round in circles until July, when a report sent from Paris arrived at the SOE headquarters in London. Graham Hayes' grave had been discovered in the Parisian cemetery in Ivry. The discovery was based on information from official French sources that also informed of the death sentence pronounced against Captain Graham Hayes for spying, his execution on the 13th of July 1943 at 16.03 hours in the 15th arrondissement in Paris and his burial in Ivry cemetery.

On the 1st of August, an SOE member was sent to the said cemetery and reported that he had no difficulty in identifying Captain Graham Hayes' grave. On the 2nd of August 1943, Graham's parents therefore received the following information from the SOE, *"There is a section of the cemetery set aside for those shot by the Germans. The graves are well looked after with flowers on every one. The greater number have a small wooden cross at the head with a shield bearing the name of the person and the date on which they were shot. At the foot of each grave is a small 'Croix de Lorraine'.*

The exact position of Captain Graham Hayes' grave is: 40 Division, 47 line, N°6".

In 1947, Graham's parents travelled to France to visit the graves of their sons Graham and Malcolm in Ivry and Saumur. In Normandy, they met with members of the de Brunville family, at their château in Asnières-en-Bessin and then with Suzanne Septavaux and Emmanuel Des Georges in Le Pin, with whom they had exchanged correspondence the previous year. Mr and Mrs Hayes wanted to personally thank them for the help and support they had offered to Graham during the war. It was during these meetings that they learned of the treachery of *Raoul*, the man who was largely responsible for their son's arrest.

On their return home, they drafted a summary of the information gathered from the many people they had met with in Normandy, and sent a copy to the SOE on the 20th of September 1947.

Simultaneously to the Hayes family's endeavours to reconstitute the memory of Graham's movements in France, the population of the town of Linton decided to build a village hall, in remembrance of the seven local sons who had lost their lives serving their country during the Second World War. An article published in the **Yorkshire Post** in February 1946 announced the construction of this place of remembrance:

*"**A village Memorial***

The little community of Linton, near Wetherby, have decided to build a village hall in Tudor style as a memorial to the seven sons of the village who laid down their lives in the war 1939-1945. They were: Major Geoffrey Appleyard, Lieut. A.R. Cooke, Captain Graham Hayes and Captain Malcolm Hayes (brothers), Flight-Sergeant R.H. ("Bill") Heydon, and Flight-Sergeant Sydney Hilder and Flight-Sergeant William Hilder (brothers).

The Memorial Hall, at the foot of the village street leading to Wetherby, will contain an ingle nook forming a shrine in which the photographs of the seven boys will be preserved. In the forecourt will be a Garden of Rest.

A building licence has been applied for so that the work may be put in hand as soon as possible".

Aside the article, the newspaper published an artist's impression of the future hall drawn by Denis Mason Jones in January 1946, his father, an architect, having drawn up the plans. The captions precisely indicated the location of each and every room:

"1939-1946 Proposed Memorial Hall, Linton, near Wetherby.

Rest Garden forecourt with Village Hall and Cloak Rms, Ground floor. Village Parlour, Kitchenette and Refreshment Balcony on Upper floor. Billiard & Dart Rm, Boys Rm, Heating & Coals in the Basement".

Denis Jones knew Graham Hayes and Geoffrey Appleyard very well, since they had spent the best part of their childhood together in Linton, and most of their weekends rambling in the surrounding countryside or playing football. During the war, Graham and Geoffrey had encouraged him to join the Commandos, but he had preferred to maintain his post as officer in the Royal Engineers.

Since the war, Jones had kept copies of all of the press articles on the young men from the village, fallen during the war, as well as those relating to the construction of the Memorial Hall. With photographs and many other documents, he reunited, for himself and for his family, a sort of memorial album which he was happy to make available for our analysis of the British remembrance of these two members of operation Aquatint.

Based on this information, we learned, from an article published in the **Yorkshire Post** on the 8th of November 1948, that the wooden panel that was to be placed as a sort of beam above the Memorial Hall fireplace, had been engraved by a craftsman who was in fact an ex-Army officer working in Graham Hayes' old workshop in Temple Sowerby, and that it was from a piece of oak that Hayes himself had bought with the intention of carving it with his very own hands. The day before the article was published, the wooden panel had been presented and consecrated in Linton church, in the presence of civil and religious authorities, and the village inhabitants.

The long, carved solid oak panel includes an engraved caption in gilded lettering indicating the rank, identity, medals, regiment and date of death.

Under Graham Hayes' photograph, the following words can be read:

"Capt. Graham HAYES, M.C.,
of the
Border Regiment's Paratroops
Special Service Commandos
Reported missing September 1942
Killed in action July 1943".

And under Geoffrey Appleyard's photograph, the following:

"Major
John Geoffrey APPLEYARD
D.S.O., M.C. Bar
Of the R.A.S.C.
The Special Air Service Regiment
Killed in action July 1943".

The Linton Memorial Hall was finally officially inaugurated in 1953 and is still used today as a town hall.

In 1999, the memory of the two men was revived with the discovery, in the Wetherby archives, of a commemorative list comprising the names of the seven young men from Linton who had died for their country during the period 1939-1945 (Roll of Honour), and of a plastercast created by Denis Mason Jones in 1946 and depicting the British Crown Coat of Arms with a central motif with the dates "1939-1945".

The list and the engraved panel were both restored, painted and varnished, and hung on the Memorial Hall wall during a ceremony on the 9th of November 2002.

Denis Jones, one of the main craftsmen and guardians of the memory of Linton's young men lost during the war, drafted the following note, which he kindly accepted to provide us with, together with photographs of Linton Memorial Hall.

"The Linton Roll of Honour

This Roll was found in 1999 in the records of the Wetherby Parish Church. It was restored and, with the coloured Date Panel, was dedicated at the British Legion Remembrance Service in the Village Hall, 9 November 2002.

The Date Panel was made in 1946 as a model for the woodcarver who made the oak Memorial Carving and Fireplace.

Linton-on-Wharfe "Village Memorial Hall" entrance, Yorkshire, 2003. (Private collection)

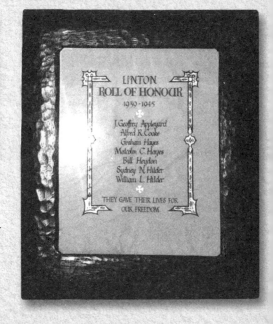

LINTON
ROLL OF HONOUR
1939 - 1945

J. Geoffrey Appleyard
Alfred R. Cooke
Graham Hayes
Malcolm C. Hayes
Bill Heydon
Sydney N. Hilder
William L. Hilder

THEY GAVE THEIR LIVES FOR
OUR FREEDOM

Photograph of the "Linton Roll of Honour, 1939-1945" created by Mr. Denis Mason Jones, 2003. (Private collection)

Portrait of **"Captain Graham Hayes, M.C."** on the wooden panel of the "Memorial Hall", 2003. (Private collection)

Interior of the Linton-on-Wharfe "Village Memorial Hall", Yorkshire, 2004. The portraits of all of the young men who lost their lives during the Second World War are displayed above the fireplace, including **Captain Graham Hayes and Major Geoffrey Appleyard.** (see photo page 12) (Private collection)

There is a poignant story about the carving.

It starts in 1936 when Graham Hayes, commemorated on the Fireplace, worked for Thompson 'the Mouseman' in Kilburn.

In 1938 he started his own workshop in Temple Sowerby and laid down, to season, a stock of English oak.

He joined the Army in 1939 and after Dunkirk he joined Geoffrey Appleyard to form one of the first raiding parties to land in France for reconnaissance and to capture prisoners.

Both were decorated for their bravery. Both were killed.

Ambushed on one raid, Graham evaded capture and was passed along the secret escape route into Spain.

There he was handed over to the Nazi Germans by a double agent.

Geoffrey avoided capture but later was shot down on a reconnaissance raid over Sicily on 13 July 1943.

On that same day Graham was executed by the Nazi Gestapo in Paris.

They were two fine men.

Their memorial was carved in the oak laid down by Graham twenty years earlier".[98]

Apparently, no specific publications have been inspired by another of the SSRF's emblematic figures, Major Gustavus March-Phillips. However, the radio programme broadcast on the BBC on the 20th of August 1971, and which was almost entirely dedicated to March-Phillips, enabled millions of British and English-speaking listeners to become aware of his existence and of his story. His daughter, Henrietta, was behind the broadcast. She was the first to speak in the script involving several voices to explain the reasons behind her quest to understand her father's true personality,

"When I was a child and my friends asked me what my father did, I used to tell them he was a pirate. In fact this was true, he was a pirate. He sailed out to Africa during the war and captured three ships. I had a picture of the boat he sailed out to Africa in, in my room. It was a sailing-boat with orange sails, sailing across a very blue sea against a very blue sky. But I never knew him, and he never even knew about me. He was killed before I was born, and my mother didn't know she was going to have a baby until after his death. Strangely enough, it was only recently that I began to want to find out about him. I was in Bristol, working in the theatre there, and one afternoon, I went into an antique shop to hire some furniture, and signed my name on the receipt and went back to the theatre. Almost immediately, there was a telephone call for me, and a voice I didn't know - a rather anxious voice - said was I by any chance related to Gus March-Phillips? I

---

[98] *Note written by **Denis Mason** Jones who produced the dated panel and who was a friend of every one of the men honoured in this **Memorial**.*

said yes, I was his daughter, and there was a sort of joyful explosion on the other end of the line. This was Tony Hall, the owner of the antique shop, and I went to see him that evening. We talked for a long time about my father, and listening to Tony, I began to think about my father for the first time as a real person, and not just a rather mythical sort of pirate. I think it was that chance meeting that really set me off on my search to discover what he was like (…)".[99]

The script was written by Henrietta, helped by Tony Hall, and based on audio recordings that she, herself, made with General Colin Gubbins, head of the SOE, of several of the operation Postmaster protagonists: Jan Nasmyth, Peter Kemp, Leonard Guise, Desmond Longe, together with the survivors from operation Aquatint: Tony Hall, Tom Winter, Tim Alleyn, Francis Howard of Penrith, and even the Anderson Manor gardener, Reginald Mullins. However, none of this would have been possible without the precious contribution of Tony Hall, ex-employee of the BBC, who had maintained extensive contacts within the famous British radio station.

During the recording which was done in a Bristol studio, witnesses came to the microphone, one after another, exchanging memories and reactions. The well adapted, and at the time very fashionable, oral style rendered the programme particularly lively.

---

[99] *Extract from the BBC programme broadcast on the 20th August 1971.*

From an editorial point of view, to our knowledge, the Aquatint raid has not been the subject of specific historical study in the UK. The operation is indeed mentioned, but only as part of the many other SSRF raids, in a few works on military history, in particular the book written by Geoffrey Appleyard's father just after the war and entitled: **Major John Geoffrey Appleyard, DSO, MC and Bar, MA of the Commandos and Special Air Service Regiment.** The operation is also mentioned in a book by Hilary St-George Saunders, **The Green Beret**, published by White Lion Publishers Limited in 1949. This book includes several place and date errors. Enthusiasts then had to await the official SOE historian, Michael Foot's account, published in 1966.

Charles Messenger accurately recalls the formation of the SSRF, after the success of operation Postmaster, in **The Commandos, 1940-1946**, published by William Kimber, London in 1985; however operation Aquatint is given very limited coverage, in view of the vastness of the topic.

On the basis of Geoffrey Appleyard's report, drafted the day after the raid, on the BBC script written in 1971 and on a few other witness accounts and sources, Mike Langley devotes a dozen pages or so to the Saint-Laurent raid in a book published in 1988, on the story of one of the members of the SSRF, Anders Lassen, who took part in operation Postmaster, but not in the raid on the 13th of September 1942. This book was, until now, the most accurate and complete work on operation Aquatint.

And finally, Ian Dear's book entitled: **Sabotage & Diversion and OSS at War**, published by Cassell, in London in 1996, together with that of Richard Brooks, published the same year and entitled: **Secret Flotillas, The Clandestine Sea Lines to France and French North Africa 1940-1944**, London, H.M.S.O., cover the essential elements already mentioned by Messenger and Langley on the Maid Honor Force and the SSRF raids, without adding any particularly new information.

The British press, on several occasions, showed a marked interest in the commando activities during the Second World War particularly at major anniversaries of the D-Day landings in Normandy. Leslie Wright, who was nicknamed "Red" by his comrades, gave certain newspapers from the "Times"[100] group several opportunities to inform their readers of the raids carried out by Major March-Phillips' men in Normandy and the Channel Islands, during his pilgrimages to Normandy to celebrate the fortieth and fiftieth anniversaries of the D-Day landings. He told them of his presence during operation Postmaster on the Island of Fernando Po on the 14th of January 1942,

---

[100] *We invite readers to consult the article: "Red's Daring Escapades on the High Seas", in **Times Group Newspaper**, Thursday, March 22, 1984, as well as that of Alicia Vella: "Secret Agent's Battle for the D-Day Bridge", in Times Group **Newspaper**, Thursday, May 12, 1994. The latter includes two photographs of Leslie Wright, one of them next to the Polish officer Roman Zawadski, brought back to England during operation **Basalt**.*

and operation Jubilee on Dieppe on the 19th of August 1942. He did not take part in operation Aquatint.

One of the most quality and highly documented press articles on the SSRF raids is that of Ian Dear, an ex-Royal Marines officer specialised in Marine military history, published in 1986 and entitled "How to win the war?"[101] Whilst insisting on the Maid Honor Force's epic history, the author presents photographs of several of the SSRF commandos (Gustavus March-Phillips, Geoffrey Appleyard, Graham Hayes, Anders Lassen, Tom Winter, André Desgrange), and of the different vessels that played such an important role (the Maid Honor, the Duchessa d'Aosta, and the MTB 344).

Just like any memory, the British memory of the Second World War commandos remains selective. Apart from among a few highly specialised historians, the codename Aquatint has been totally forgotten in the United Kingdom. Denis Mason Jones, despite his great attention to the memory of the heroes from Linton, fallen in the field of honour, even admitted to André Heintz, in a letter dated the 9th of January 2004, that this codename was totally unknown to him. Postmaster, however, always arouses a keen interest, and a certain pride, as I personally was to discover when talking to one of the Public Record Office managers in Kew in the summer of 2004.

---

[101] *Unfortunately, **Leslie Wright**, who is now deceased, omitted to note the precise name and date of the newspaper on the copy of the article.*

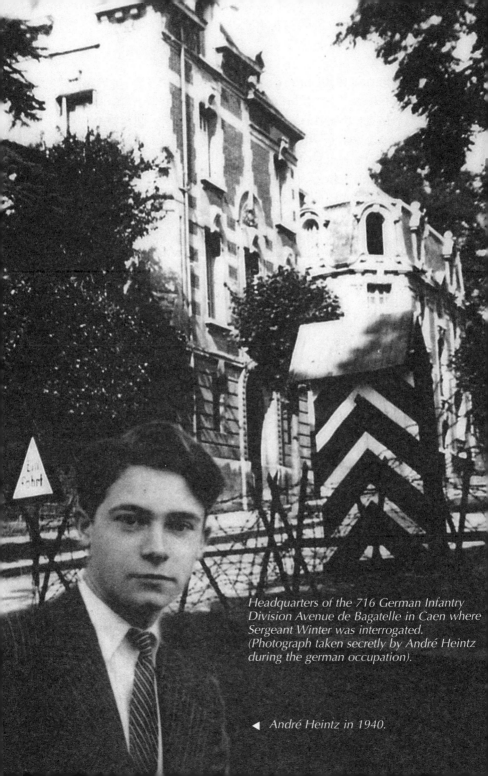

Headquarters of the 716 German Infantry Division Avenue de Bagatelle in Caen where Sergeant Winter was interrogated. (Photograph taken secretly by André Heintz during the german occupation).

◄ André Heintz in 1940.

CHAPTER III
THE PAINSTAKING REMEMBRANCE OF A RESISTANCE FIGHTER FROM CAEN

Born in Caen, in Normandy, André Heintz was a young English student in 1942 who found himself indirectly and totally fortuitously caught up in this fascinating story. A Resistance Fighter, member of the OCM (Civil and Military Organisation), and deliverer of the clandestine newspaper **"Témoignage Chrétien"** (Christian Witness), André Heintz' path was to cross, purely by chance, that of two of Aquatint's commandos (Lord Howard and Tom Winter), whom he met again forty years later. Captivated by this extraordinary and tragic wartime story, fascinated by the lives of those men of such singular destinies, André Heintz undertook more than twenty years of painstaking research, of which the publication of this book is one of the ultimate accomplishments. We owe most of the information concerning operation Aquatint (the historical documents, in English and in German, be they reports or letters) to André Heintz. I am delighted to have been able to help him to conclude this long and difficult quest for truth. And so, henceforth, the historian abandons his pen, for a few pages, to the faithful and indefatigable guardian of the memory of Aquatint:

"I had just spent my summer holidays at my grand-mother's house in the Cotentin Peninsula, when, on the 13th of September 1942, I was preparing to return home to Caen. I was on my bicycle and, to go to Carentan to take my train, I had to cross the Ponts Douve bridges that were indispensable for crossing the marshland. Strangely enough, over the centuries, at each war, these three rather insignificant bridges had acted as an obstacle, including in June 1940, when the Germans had been sufficiently hindered to enable the English troops to re-embark at Cherbourg. Since then, controls by the occupying authorities were commonplace. But, on that day, it was a veritable barrage. I was rapidly surrounded by soldiers and searched, while two of them checked my identity papers, another asked me what I was carrying and tried to take a book out of my front satchel. I was immediately worried for, at the time, I was preparing a "memoir" in English on Kipling and my English books, including my French-English dictionary, were all in my satchel. It would have been ridiculous to get into trouble for just that. Thankfully, short of space, I had sufficiently cramped the books into the satchel that the soldier didn't manage to extract a single one of them and he contented himself with my explanations.

Intrigued by the extraordinary strictness of the control (if my memory serves me well, the soldier who spoke very good French, even asked me for the names of my parents and my grandparents), I took the risk of asking one of the soldiers what was going on. He declared outright, and in a grave manner, "Tommies landed!" I had trouble not bursting out laughing, for, so close to the coast, if the much-awaited landing had taken place, I reckoned we would have noticed something. However, just as serious as before, the German repeated, "Tommies landed!" I didn't believe a word of it.

And it all ended there. I took my train without further incident.

As soon as I arrived in Caen, I met with my university friends. A few days later one of them, a medical student, told me, "You should come with me, you speak English; at the hospital, there are two English soldiers who appear to be having problems. There's a sentry guard at their door on a permanent basis; we'll get in via the back garden and, since their room is on the ground floor, we'll be able to see them from the window".

So what was said was duly done, however, to our disappointment, one of the soldiers waved to us to leave and, since we insisted, he repeated his dissuasive and commanding gesture. The other soldier, who was lying in his bed, didn't move; he was as pale as death.[102] The one who was chasing us away was awkwardly seated in a very uncomfortable armchair, with one of his legs stretched out. It was evident that this giant of a man was suffering.[103]

I didn't for a second think there could be a link between these two wounded soldiers and the "Tommies landed". Furthermore, the Resistance regularly asked me to come to talk to airmen who had been ejected from their planes, or to escapees, to offer them moral support, or simply to confirm that they were, in fact, English.

I always tried to forget as quickly as possible, for, at the time, it was more prudent to train oneself into forgetfulness which, in reality, one did not always control.

It was only some years after the war that it all came back up to the surface.

In the 50's, I read with much enthusiasm, a first book on the British Commando activities which had been given to me by its author, Sir Hilary St-George Saunders, a House of Commons librarian. In fact, Mr Daure, rector of the University of Caen, taking advantage of one of my trips to England, had asked me to deliver a message to him. I was very warmly welcomed in this prestigious location, at a period in history when the word Caen was almost a password. Sir Hilary had been one of the first

---

[102] *The reader will realise that this is Lieutenant Tony Hall, seriously wounded and left such a long time inert on the beach that an inhabitant of Saint-Laurent thought there were four dead bodies.*

[103] *In view of the nature of his wounds and his stature, this was clearly Lord Howard of Penrith.*

men to enter into the town of Caen in 1944 and he told me, "Such a shame we didn't meet earlier; you wouldn't have left me to sleep outside, would you, just like I had to on my first night in Caen!"

It was in his book that I learned that a few commandos, that had been so frequently spoken of at the time of the Normandy D-Day landings had actually already secretly landed on our coastline during the Occupation. Hence, I learned that they had come to Houlgate, to Bruneval, to Barfleur, to Les Casquets, to Sark... But certain deformed place names were difficult to locate, such as: "Pointe de Forli, near "Cape Barfleur" (sic) which I did eventually manage to associate with "Pointe de Fouly" 4 miles to the south of Barfleur. However "St-Honoré", close to the "Cherbourg Peninsula" (sic) remained an enigma, even after the discovery of a document recounting a raid at "Sainte-Honorine-des-Pertes".

My friend, Jean Collin, General Secretary at the university rectorate simultaneously to Mr Daure's reign as rector, introduced me to the Sainte-Honorine school teacher, who had occupied the job for over 25 years, and who, as coincidence would have it, was in fact his sister! She certified that there had never been a raid at Sainte-Honorine during the Occupation and that, furthermore, she had never even heard of incursions in the region. So the mystery remained.

Independently, after the death of my parents in the 70's, I developed a certain attraction to cemeteries and paid visit to those small rural cemeteries whose entrance was marked by a plaque indicating: "COMMON-WEALTH WAR GRAVES COMMISSION". I had paid particular attention to Saint-Laurent-sur-Mer cemetery, hidden behind the trees beside the church, and hosting three British graves; the grave belonging to a certain Leonard had particularly intrigued me, for, at the base of the headstone, where one can generally read a prayer or an inscription suggested by the family, there was a text in German. It was the first two lines of "L'Internationale"! (Communist anthem by Eugène Pottier). The locals had told me that there had been a Frenchman in the group, and that perhaps he was Leonard, but that was totally illogical; why would there be a text in German? Other locals told me, "The Frenchman was taken prisoner and, as he was taken away, he shouted, "Don't worry, we'll be back!" So, it couldn't be him.

I still had no reason to make the connection between this raid and the said St-Honoré raid. Even if it had, in fact, taken place at Sainte-Honorine, less than 3 miles from Saint-Laurent, the dates didn't coincide. The dates of death inscribed on the graves were the 12th of September, for two of them, and the 13th of September for Leonard - yet another peculiarity, for Sir Hilary mentioned the night of the 7th to 8th of September in his book.

At this stage, I was at a dead-end. Then, several years went by before part of the mysterious cloud finally started to dissipate, not purely by chance, but not the way I expected it to either.

On the 40th anniversary of the D-Day landings in 1984, Dr Duncombe, one of my scouting mates from 1935 to 1938, called me to explain that, as Deputy Mayor of Caen, he was snowed under by the various commemorative ceremonies and that he was no longer able to look after a commando who was staying at his house. Since the veteran was unable to offer himself a hotel room, Franck Duncombe asked me if I could put him up. My wife immediately agreed.

Once the ceremonies were over, this brave man expressed his keenness to visit his old wartime chief's grave. He told me that he had been killed during a raid on the coast, but that he didn't know the precise location.

And when Leslie Wright, for that was the veteran's name, explained to me that his commander was Major March-Phillips, I immediately realised that his grave was one of those in the Saint-Laurent village cemetery. I finally and very probably held one of the keys to the great mystery. It was already quite surprising to find British graves in the American sector of Omaha Beach where so many Americans had fallen in 1944. But what role had these British soldiers played in 1942, and who was Leonard?

Unfortunately, or rather fortunately for him, Leslie Wright had not taken part in the raid and he knew nothing of this pseudo-German. However, he was not at all surprised at his presence within the group which, he explained to me, had comprised a number of foreign members.

Leslie Wright had joined the "Force", as he called it, at its very foundation, and he told us fascinating stories like, for example, one of their first exploits during which, just like pirates, they had captured two enemy ships. On the onset, their mission consisted of exploring the West African coastline in search of Italian or German vessels on special missions, or to hunt down German military ships that came to refuel in neutral ports. The commando sailed in a sailing trawler, equipped with two engines and well-hidden armaments. To capture the two boats, they used all sorts of cunning: the crew of both vessels were invited to a reception while their ships disappeared. In order to instantaneously cut the mooring ropes, frogmen were sent on reconnaissance to identify the size of the anchor chain links. The men who were to capture the boats withdrew into the desert with similar links and tried various explosives to determine the necessary charge to break the chains. These men, who had been enlisted to perpetrate sabotage missions, and who, until then, had remained frustrated, revelled in such exercises. Leslie Wright told us, "We had a great lark". When the explosion finally occurred, the Italian officer who had been invited to the dinner party, immediately realised the treachery and cried, "Oh, the bastards!"

With such nostalgia that it was almost as if he had returned there, Leslie Wright also spoke of Anderson Manor where the group had resumed quarters upon his return to England to continue their training. It was an Elizabethan manor house situated within a magnificent estate. Leslie appeared to have spent the happiest days of his life there, despite the harshness of the exercises: firing, sabotage, close combat, navigation, day and night marches. There was the most extraordinary sense of camaraderie. But, they all impatiently awaited their next mission. To abate their fervour, the officers let them look after the maintenance of the estate; together with the manor house's gardener, they gathered hay, grew vegetables, etc…

Before leaving, Leslie promised that he would introduce me to one of the survivors of the Saint-Laurent raid, his old Sergeant, Tom Winter.

Concurrently, I tried to consult documents that might enlighten me on the Commando raids from the British National Archives at the Public Record Office (PRO) in Kew, not far from London. At the time, the filing of such documents remained somewhat disorderly. However, I did manage to get my hands on a document concerning the "Sainte-Honorine raid", but it was far from complete. Indeed, the raid's survivors didn't come home until after the war. The report had been drafted based on the explosions that had been heard and the lights that had been seen from the speedboat whilst awaiting, in vain, the return of its crew.

One day when I was in London, Leslie invited me to his home together with his old Sergeant. For Tom Winter, who was already aged, the trip from the Isle of Wight to London was already quite an expedition, but both men were keen to exchange their memories and Leslie was proud to show Tom the picture he had painted of their "pirate ship": the Maid Honor. During this first meeting with Tom Winter, he remained very reserved and said little of his great deeds. I hardly learned anything about Postmaster, which was the codename for their African mission, or even about Aquatint, the said Sainte-Honorine raid. However, I did learn from Tom that, during the operation, a Lord, who was one of the group members, was in charge of the light embarkation which had taken them to the beach. When they had tried to retreat, the Lord had been wounded, was taken prisoner and sent to hospital in Caen where Tom Winter, also a prisoner, had been confronted with him one day by the Germans.

Tom Winter encouraged me to meet this Lord and he gave me his address. He was Lord Howard of Penrith from Cirencester (close to the Welsh border).

At the time, I was close to retirement and was renovating an old farmhouse built by monks in the 15th Century at Valjoie, in the vicinity of Gavray. I had managed to have Gavray twinned with a small English town close to Oxford. On one of my trips to England, I told the Chairman of the twinning committee, with whom I was staying, about this Lord. He immediately replied, "We're less than 50 miles from his estate, I'll take you there if you like". I couldn't believe my ears. I think he was just as keen as I was to meet this Lord! Of course, he took the trouble to call first, after having consulted the Who's Who which gave us, not only his address and tele-phone number, but also his biography.

Lord Howard was very understanding and, despite the fact that he was busy with his wife organising a garden party for the Church of England, he was ready to welcome us.

When we arrived at the castle farm, we found a tall, strong, but limping man, because of his leg injury. He lived in great simplicity; he and his wife were a fine example of ecumenism, he himself being a Catholic and his wife an Anglican, both helping each other, and without doubt highly respected and appreciated by the entire village to which they demonstrated devotion and generosity.

I informed Lord Howard that it was, in fact, the second time I had seen him and explained the circumstances and the attempts to make contact with him when he was in hospital in Caen. He hesitated a moment, astonished, then declared, "I'm going to explain to you; I'm sorry to have chased you away, but you'll understand why. One day, shortly after I had been taken to hospital with Tony Hall, who was still unconscious, the Germans came rummaging around in my room and told me that I had a visitor. And, indeed, they then brought Sergeant Winter. And, much to my surprise, they left us alone. Suspecting that the Germans had placed microphones, I signalled as best I could to Tom Winter to say as little as possible. The Germans had set a trap. Since Winter and Boatswain Desgrange from the Free French Naval Forces were the only ones, together with ourselves, to have been taken prisoner, the Germans were convinced that there were other commandos who had escaped but they didn't know how many. During the interrogations that we had endured, we had all refused to give any further information than our name and our regimental number. By leaving us alone, they thought we would come to talk of our comrades".

"So you now know", he added, "why we had to stay on our guard, and we had had enough trouble already; that's why we chased you away".

Lord Howard told me that Tom had been very brave, for during the following interrogations, he had been particularly cruelly treated. Tom had also been forced to caution the Frenchman, Desgrange, for he tended to boast and to talk too much!

With Lord Howard, we talked about the Saint-Laurent graves, in particular Leonard's. I then learned that he was a Czech and that his daughter lived in London.

All the mysteries started to become clearer.

I also learned that March-Phillips, the commander, had a daughter who also lived in London and that it would be interesting to locate her.

There again, in this fountain of coincidences, I struck lucky. In 1935, when I was 14, I had been educated in an English school in Bristol for 6 months. I admit to having regularly thought of my British friends during the Occupation; I envied them for being able to freely fight the enemy, whilst we, ourselves, were reduced to clandestine tactics. In 1954, I was fortunate to exchange jobs with one of the grammar school's teachers and, since we had kept in touch afterwards, I one day told him about the Saint-Laurent raid and that one of the commandos had been hit on the head and totally knocked out by a German with a stick grenade. My colleague interrupted me and said,

"That story sounds a lot like my friend's; he's an antique dealer and remained hemiplegic after a similar wound received during a raid on the French coast. He's away at the moment, but I'll find out more as soon as he's home".

Shortly afterwards, I was surprised to receive a magnificent letter from Tony Hall, demonstrating his unyielding optimism. This man, who had remained handicapped his entire life from the wounds received on our soil, ended his letter with the moving phrase "Vive la France!"

I learned that the aim of the raid was to bring back information, but also to capture prisoners,

"When," he told me, *"we found ourselves at odds with the patrol, I managed to grab onto one of the Germans and drag him to the boat when another soldier I hadn't noticed clobbered me on the back of the head with a stick grenade. I lost consciousness".*

So it was indeed Tony Hall that I had seen, motionless, next to Lord Howard in Caen hospital in 1942. We now know how Tony Hall, who had always been fascinated by objets d'art had, with great courage and skill, opened his antique store in Bristol, despite his hemiplegia.

The pieces of the puzzle started to fit together, but there was more to come!

Tony told me, "One day when I returned to the store after going shopping, I thought I heard someone say the name "March-Phillips". When I checked the delivery book, I did indeed find an order for old furniture for the Old Vic theatre in Bristol; an order that had been signed by Henrietta March-Phillips. My heart skipped a jump, and I leapt to the telephone. This hyphenated name was most uncommon in England and I immediately suspected a possible family link. I had trouble getting in touch with her. I was very impatient. When I finally managed to speak to her, she told me that she was, indeed, my ex-commander, March-Phillips' daughter. But, her lacking eagerness was contradictory to my own enthusiasm!

However, I couldn't help but tell her of my great admiration and affection for her father. I mentioned a few of the events we had experienced together and even some of his character traits, the respect that his men had for him, for example when in the barracks-room, this practicing Catholic got down on his knees to say his evening prayer. We'd never seen that before, especially in England where Catholics were a minority and not always particularly well looked upon.

However, I was soon forced into silence for, at the other end of the line, Henrietta was crying. Before hanging up, I said to her "We must meet!" "

Tony Hall kept his word and he had realised the

extent to which his telephone call had deeply moved Henrietta March-Phillips, born several months after her father's death.

She, who had never shown the slightest interest in her father, was now eager to learn more about him.

Tony Hall also realised that he had experienced, together with his prestigious commander, quite uncommon events worthy of a motion picture. He remembered his prior professional activities which consisted in putting together radio programmes, and advised Henrietta to contact the raids' survivors and to record their witness accounts. Tony already saw the potential of a radio broadcast on the subject. The BBC showed an interest in his idea and a script was written.

Tony gave me Henrietta's address and I met with her later in London. This young girl, who had become a mature and delicate woman, admitted to me that before her meeting with Tony Hall, she had never felt the slightest affection for the father she had never known.

"The reason, she added, "that I burst into tears at Tony Hall's first phone call, was that, as I listened to him, I was overwhelmed with guilt, guilt at having despised such a hero and at never having loved a man who had been so venerated by all those who had come close to him".

Before we separated, Henrietta offered me a copy of the script she had written for the BBC, with Tony Hall's help.

Nothing could have helped me more in my discovery of all of these men. As I read the text, it was as if I had met them, listened to them, discovered their personalities, even their funny little habits.

I learned that March-Phillips was lively and so short-tempered that he tended to stutter, but no-one would ever have dreamed of making fun of him.

Just like Appleyard, he had fought at Dunkirk. They both loved nature. When March-Phillips spoke of nature, he was almost a poet; he had written three novels. Tony Hall enjoyed philosophising and had a great sense of humour. The group's Frenchman, André Desgrange was a chatty, lively chap. All of these men, or almost all of them, loved the sea. They admitted to often being afraid, but they knew how to overcome their fear, and that was where their true bravery lay!

So we had found Captain Lord Howard, Lieutenant Tony Hall and Sergeant Tom Winter, and we knew where the three other commando members' graves were: Leonard's, who in fact was a Czech and whose real name was Lehniger, Major March-Phillips' and Sergeant Alan Williams', the youngest of the commando members who had lost his life at the age of 22. We also knew that Boatswain André Desgrange had been taken prisoner, just like Tom Winter. However, the raid reports mentioned eleven men: six officers, two sergeants and three privates. So what had happened to Captain Burton and Privates Hellings and Orr?

Tom Winter gave me Burton's address in South Africa, where he had retired. However, it was his widow who answered my letter; unfortunately her husband, John, had died the previous year, but she explained to me, *"John was one of the unlucky ones to be left behind. He, a Pole and a Dutchman, were swimming towards the boat when it had to leave because of heavy gunfire. The 3 of them swam down the coast for a bit and then went ashore. They hoped to walk to the Spanish border, but found out after they were caught that they had been going round in circles! I can't remember how many days they were wandering around, but they got food and clothes from the French people"*. They ended up prisoners.

So, our enquiry was progressing, since we now knew the fate of the three escapees and that Orr was probably Polish and Hellings Dutch.

I was soon to meet with Wing Commander Brian Spray, ex-military attaché from the British Embassy in Paris and a friend of Mme de Falandre, whom I will talk of much of later. The Admiralty had given him a brief report on the raid. The report claimed that the listening post in Barfleur had located the boat and had alerted the defence posts along the entire coast. So the Germans were waiting for them.

This was, however, contradictory to witness accounts from the inhabitants of Saint-Laurent.

"After the raid," they recalled, "a limping German guard dog was seen rambling around with an Iron Cross round his neck. He had been decorated for having detected the commando".

It was also said, in Saint-Laurent, that two villagers had been requisitioned to drag up to the top of the beach the bodies of three commandos who had been killed or drowned; the locals had built coffins from the shutters and floorboards of abandoned houses. No-one had been allowed to take part in the funeral ceremony, but they knew that the Germans had fired a three gun salute as the coffins were lowered into their graves, on approximately the same spot as they can be seen today; at the time a simple wooden cross marked the spot.

I finally learned that the de Brunville family from the Château d'Asnières, situated further inland near Vierville, had accommodated one of the commandos who had been brought to them by M Lemasson, a nearby farmer. Could it be one of the escapees, or perhaps Captain Hayes of whom I knew nothing at this stage?

I managed to meet with Olivier de Brunville who explained how he had driven Hayes to Bayeux and handed him over to Mr Humann from Juaye-Mondaye. We now know that Mr Humann then took Hayes by train from Bayeux to Lisieux, from where he was driven to Le Pin.

The story then became far more complicated, particularly since Graham Hayes was to be the victim of treachery.

Olivier de Brunville introduced me to his sister Mme de Falandre (née Isabelle de Brunville), who had kept the various letters that the Hayes family had sent to her parents, including the SOE reports collected throughout their research.

From all of this correspondence, transpired a multitude of endeavours and verifications and the immense despair of a family totally unable to find out what had become of their son. For a long time, they had been convinced that they would find him in a concentration camp in Germany, a hypothesis that had been further supported by the account by Flight Lieutenant JEC Evans who, on his return from captivity, had told them of their simultaneous detention in Fresnes prison.

There were still so many mysteries to be resolved concerning Graham.

Who was the traitor? What role did the pseudo resistant who took him to the Spanish border play? Did he even go that far? Were the letters and messages used as evidence false? Why and how did Hayes go back to Fresnes after having reached Spain?

One of Mme de Falandre's letters indicated that Graham's grave had been located in Ivry. Wing Commander Brian Spray went to Ivry to check and reported back that the wooden cross carried the inscription: "Gream (sic) Hayes" thus misspelling his name.

As if compelled by some mysterious intuition, Brian Spray decided to return to Ivry cemetery to consult the registry. As the cemetery caretaker handed the registry to him, a letter fell to the floor. The caretaker rushed to pick it up but the Wing Commander insisted on reading its contents; he had noticed the Royal Coat of Arms which adorned all official documents. The letter informed of the transfer of Graham Hayes' grave to Viroflay cemetery on the 1st of May 1951! So, Brian Spray went to Viroflay where, indeed, he found Graham's grave. So Captain Hayes now had two graves! Clearly the entire story was to be full of surprises, but we hadn't yet seen the last of them.

The most astonishing surprise was yet to come…

When I taught at Caen University, giving lessons to foreign students, I regularly organised excursions which could include students from up to fifteen or so different nationalities. One day, on our return from such an excursion on the D-Day landing beaches, a German student came to ask for my help.

"I have", he told me, "a free subject to study for my German university. I've chosen the French Resistance. Could you help me?" I was quite embarrassed because, for as far as the Germans were concerned, the Resistance had comprised only vile spies, if not "terrorists". But this young German appeared to already be well informed. He was an enthusiastic Francophile and was even engaged to a young girl from Caen. And in any case, he was far from belonging to the Nazi generation. So I decided to give him some information and also sent him to see some of my old Resistance comrades. At the end of term, he returned home to Freiburg (Freiburg im Breisgau in Bade-Wurtemberg).

He came back to Caen at Easter to see his fiancée, and paid me a visit. He brought with him an impressive pile of photocopied documents and said, "I remembered that during the Occupation, you lived close to the staff headquarters of the 716th Infantry Division, the one that covered the entire British coastal landing zone in 1944. I thought maybe these documents would interest you. However, I'm afraid you may be somewhat disappointed for they hardly mention the Resistance. There are only two references: one indirectly suspecting the Resistance, the day of the military parade organised for General Matterstock's departure (he was to be replaced by General Richter) when a British bomber strafed the ceremony; the other concerned a map copier employed by the Staff to copy all of its maps. He was suspected of systematically making an extra copy which he sent to the 2nd Bureau in Vichy, the Air Information Department. However, someone from Vichy, clearly at odds with the copier, had the audacity to send one of the maps back to the Staff advising them to keep an eye on the person who copied their documents. Then the Gestapo got involved and we don't know how the story ended…"

I replied to the young German, "Alas, I know the story; the copier was Henri Brunet who was executed after a lengthy court case, and I know his family. He left his wife and a very young child".

I continued to leaf through the precious document which covered the Staff activities from 1942 to the end of May 1944. I was particularly disappointed that it did not cover the D-Day landing period, but it was a masterpiece of German perfectionism. For each and every day, 4 items were covered: 1 The weather, 2 The Staff activities, 3 The attitude of the local population and 4 Enemy activity (often left blank since in 1942 there was very little enemy activity).

I was far from imagining that I was on the verge of making a major discovery. As I continued to leaf through the pages, I finally came to a section that was no longer separated into items; it was more of a continuous narration, only punctuated by a few maps. It clearly concerned a coastal zone; it indicated the direction of gunfire from fortified bases called: WN 29a, 29b, 29c, the high sea line and the time: Hochflut um 23.25 Uhr, the approach of a boat indicated by a dotted line, three black marks on the beach with the inscription "3 tote Engländer" (3 dead Englishmen). My German was limited but sufficient for me to make the connection with the unfortunate raid at Saint-Laurent. Finally, my suspicions were confirmed; the last map mentioned Saint-Laurent and the date of the 13th of September 1942.

My young German student was far from imagining that he had just brought me the most precious document I could ever have hoped to possess, and that no-one, up to now, had been able to unearth. The 20 page, highly detailed report offered us a mine of information, as well as the advantage of possessing the original German version of events. After reading the report, it was clear that the poor British soldiers had no chance of making it. Without knowing it, they had fallen directly within a particularly well defended zone, by 1942 standards, with several guns and search lights. Furthermore, their arrival coincided with two German patrols, one on its way back to base, the other beginning its round. Right from the start they had two patrols after them! Judging by the number of waistbelts found in the boat and on the beach, the Germans had deduced that there were eleven commandos, but they had supposed that most of them had drowned rather than escaped, particularly since they were convinced that they had sunk the speedboat.

I also learned that Tony Hall, dazed by a grenade, had also been injured by shrapnel from another grenade, hence his arm wound: furthermore, the soldier that Hall had hung onto was called Kowalski. This explains why he shouted to Hall, "nicht Deutsch! nicht Deutsch! Czechich!", to which Hall replied, "Give me a break, we'll sort that out in the boat!"

The maps contained in the German report clearly proved that the last body, Richard Lehniger's, had in fact been washed up by the sea, and that he had drowned and not been massacred.

I had already met with his widow and his daughter in London, and had been deeply moved by this family who had been continuously tortured by the fear that the Germans discover his Jewish origins. He had also served in the Austro-Hungarian army and had escaped from a state annexed by Germany. The discovery on the German map enabled me to reassure his family on the circumstances of his death, and I gave them a copy in support of my findings.

More and more people became interested in this episode of the secret war. The inhabitants of Saint-Laurent began to appreciate the importance of this "pinprick" to the Atlantic wall. The scale of the American landings on their beach in 1944 had led them to almost totally forget the 1942 raid. It was however, a direct response to one of Churchill's ideas, *"to harass the Germans and oblige them to maintain troops on the West coast"*, also demanded by Stalin who constantly called for "the opening of a second front" to alleviate his own.

Our own research was progressing. We had found three survivors, Major Lord Howard of Penrith, Tony Hall and Tom Winter, as well as the widow and the daughter of Gustavus March-Phillips, the widow and daughter of Richard Lehniger, John Burton's trace, however, hardly any information on the Frenchman André Desgrange. I had even tried to write to him in Angers, where Henrietta had interviewed him, but received no reply. As yet, we knew nothing about Adam Orr and Jan Hellings, neither concerning their captivity nor even if they had survived the war.

I was in touch with two British historians who were both busy writing books on the Commandos: Mike Langley was writing Anders Lassen's story; one of the SSRF's Swedish members. Lassen had not taken part in operation Aquatint, but had participated in other raids with the same commandos. Fascinated by the raid, he wanted to explain how its failure had modified the course of Anders Lassen's career.

The second historian, Charles Messenger was retracing the entire Commando story and wanted to give precise details concerning the Saint-Laurent tragedy. I think it was Leslie Wright who suggested that he write to me. Together, we exchanged our discoveries as and when we made them. Langley surprised me by sending Adam Orr's death certificate on which was written: "after 12th March 1945". Moreover, Mike Langley had discovered that Orr was in fact called Opoczynski.

However, concerning Jan Hellings, we had all come to a dead end; the Commonwealth War Graves Commission had given us information on several graves of the same name, but none of them seemed to belong to our Jan Hellings.

I, of course, informed Mme de Falandre of my findings, for she had, from the very beginning, shown a great interest in the fate of Graham Hayes. However, I could sense her great disappointment at no longer having any contact with the Hayes family. Many years had gone by; Lilian and Herbert Hayes were both deceased and no-one in Kiln Hill, in Linton, replied any more. I had told Henrietta and she attempted an ad in the classified column of the Times, without success.

In addition, Mrs Davidson, who had received visits from Graham during his stay in Garches, now lived in England in the same town as one of my friends, an ex-assistant at Malherbe High School in Caen. I called him and he confirmed that her address was close to his own and he offered to help. Unfortunately, the person who had been living in the house for the last thirty years had lost contact with Mrs Davidson.

Mme de Falandre had kept in touch with the survivors of the Le Pin group. Mme Nicole Duval, whose father, Dr Hautechaud had died during deportation and whose mother had been arrested and had disappeared, often said to Mme de Falandre, "I'd like to know if Graham Hayes embroidered; among the English that my parents had helped, there was one who did needlework; I doubt it could've been Graham, since it's quite rare for a fighting man to take to embroidery, but, if I saw a photograph of him, I'm sure I would recognise him".

So we firstly needed to find out if there were still any descendants from the Hayes family, and then we needed to fathom out the sad story of the treachery that was to lead to Graham Hayes' death. Kieffer's role in the story was already clear, but the role played by the pseudo resistant who took him to the Spanish border remained a mystery. Even his name was spelled in a variety of ways: "Hortet" with or without the "H" and also "Orkl". A young history teacher, Gérard Fournier became interested in the affair; he was already an avid archive researcher and had published a long article on the Resistance activities in collaboration with the SOE in the Lisieux region.[104]

At the same time, I maintained contact with the SOE adviser. He helped us to find the French members of this

---

[104] *Gérard Fournier, "Il y a 50 ans, le pasteur Orange rentrait de déportation", Information and Liaison* **Bulletin** *n° 5,* **Calvados Departmental Archives,** *1995*

British network, in order to put together a CD-Rom on the History of the Resistance in Calvados.

At the time, the adviser was busy exploring the last of the SOE archives in order to select those he was to send to the Public Record Office. During one of our discussions, I spoke to him about Aquatint and he had been particularly attentive to the case of Graham Hayes. He had even, at one point, considered writing a book or a screenplay. I informed him of my own personal research and he very kindly complemented our own information concerning Kieffer and Ortet, as far as his mandatory respect of professional secrecy would permit.

In 1985, I had almost brought my research to a close. Since we now knew all of the remaining survivors of the raid, as well as the families of two of the commandos buried at Saint-Laurent, Mme de Falandre and I considered it was time to organise a commemorative ceremony on the 13th of September. Until then, a wreath had been laid on the three graves on the 11th of November each year, but no commemoration had ever taken place on the raid's anniversary date. The families had, of course, never been invited. Mme de Falandre and I did our best to convince the Mayor, M Mahieu. He immediately saw the interest in our project since he had lived in Saint-Laurent at the time of the raid. He chose the Sunday that was closest to the anniversary date of the 13th of September and invited the local authorities to the ceremony. M and Mme Chedal-Anglay helped Mme de Falandre to organise the commemoration.

It was decided to repeat the ceremony the following year and to invite all of our contacts in England, as well as a maximum of other personalities. Following the death of M Mahieu in June, this proved to be a major task for the new Mayor, M Martin, however, the ceremony turned out to be a great success. The village was proud to

▲
Mme de Falandre and Olivier de Brunville standing next to Wing Commander Brian Spray, at M and Mme Chedal-Anglay's home in *Vierville-sur-Mer, 21ˢᵗ September 1985. (Chedal-Anglay Collection)*

commemorate its heroes and to welcome the families who had given so much for their freedom. We were also delighted to see Mme Duval honoured; she who, for over 40 years, had so terribly suffered from the disappearance of her parents.

M Martin then showed a marked interest in the Commando operations, to such an extent that he drafted a brochure summarising their history and their activities throughout the world.

In 1994, Leslie Wright came back to France with his friend Tom Winter, who was becoming weaker and weaker. We realised that it would very probably be the old Sergeant's last visit. However, it was also the opportunity to learn of the immense joy he had experienced when, a few years previously, he had participated in the routine control of Les Casquets Lighthouse. Setting foot once more on the rocks of Les Casquets brought back so many memories and was such a fine achievement. For Tom, it had been the most prized reward he could ever have dreamed of: what a great accomplishment it was for him to have managed to jump onto that rock again at the age of 85!

In 1996, Duncan Stuart, the SOE advisor who had already so kindly helped us, was to offer us the most precious of surprises; the one that was to deeply move Mme de Falandre; he announced that he had tracked down the youngest of the Hayes children: Austen.

He had left his native Yorkshire to settle in the magnificent Somerset countryside. He lived in a quiet and picturesque village, close to Nether Stowey, where the romantic poet Coleridge had written some of his most exquisite verses. Austen lived among a group of artists; he had inherited his family's artistic talent.

Austen wrote a long letter to Mme de Falandre in which he spoke of himself and of his brother, and enclosed a photograph of Graham. Mme de Falandre rushed to show the photograph to Mme Duval who was immediately thrilled. She recognised Graham; he was indeed the man who had sewn the embroidery!

Towards the end of her life, Mme Duval considerately offered the precious embroidery to Mme de Falandre; Austen had explained the different allegories it contained.

Austen was not keen on the idea of coming to Normandy, much to the disappointment of these ladies who wanted to know everything about his brother Graham. I was familiar with the region of Somerset where Austen lived and had several friends there to whom I paid regular visits. The town of Bristol, where I had studied, was also nearby. Since I was planning to take part, exceptionally, in the school's annual former student reunion, I decided to pay a visit to my friends in Somerset immediately afterwards. My hostess, Mrs Field considerately invited Austen to her home during my short stay. He bombarded me with questions and I told him of the great lengths to which we had gone to find him, in particular the ad that Henrietta March-Phillips had had published in the Times. He was aware of the ad, but had not read it himself. His friends who had seen it only spoke to him about it some time later and they, unfortunately, had not kept a copy. It was too late to reply.

Austen spoke about his brother. In fact, with the war and their eight year age difference, they had hardly known each other. What's more, his elder brother intimidated him; he had so much more experience. Austen told me of how terribly proud he was the day, in their family home in Linton, his brother Graham invited him into his bedroom to show him his collection of stuffed animals, birds in particular.

I, of course, went to great lengths to persuade Austen to come to Normandy. And he did indeed come to the following year's commemorative ceremony. He was given the warmest of welcomes by those who had awaited his visit for such a long time. He was also accompanied by Duncan Stuart at the reception organised by M and Mme Chedal-Anglay.

▲
Austen Hayes (right) and Duncan Stuart (centre) conversing with Mme de Falandre at M and Mme Chedal-Anglay's home on the 12th of September 1997. (Chedal-Anglay Collection)

Unfortunately, three years later, no-one had any news of Austen. I had not received my traditional Christmas Card. It was worrying. The British respect that tradition so religiously, that, when they fail to receive a card from one of their friends, they immediately conclude, "either my friend's died or he's cross with me!" In our case, it turned out to be the first reason. No-one answered the phone anymore and I knew no-one else in his village. It was finally Mrs Field who managed to confirm to us that Austen had died; as an artist, she knew his group of fellow painters and called one of them who replied, "Alas, our friend Austen passed away just before Christmas; we are all at a loss, we miss him so much".

So the long chapter had almost come to a close. So many mysteries, so many coincidences, so many encounters since that 13th of September 1942. The further I progressed, the more convinced I was that the protagonists of the Aquatint raid were worthy of celebrity. It was a duty to pay homage to their courage and their sacrifice, and that's precisely what we had done.

CHAPTER IV
THE NORMANDY REMEMBRANCE
OF *AQUATINT*

What mark did Aquatint leave in the memories of the Normandy people?

When we take a closer look, we can distinguish three categories of collective Norman and French remembrance of operation Aquatint: the private memory of witnesses, the official remembrance among local and national authorities and the associative remembrance.

The private memory of witnesses only concerns a few rare inhabitants of Saint-Laurent-sur-Mer and Vierville-sur-Mer, since the Germans had very rapidly controlled, then forbidden access to the landing zone, thus preventing any contact with the victims and the escapees.

As from 1985, a new form of remembrance has emerged among the official French authorities, essentially among the successive Mayors and town councillors from Saint-Laurent, who since then have organised annual commemorations in honour of the British commandos who died during operation Aquatint.

And finally, although they were not personally witnesses to the 1942 events, several inhabitants from Saint-Laurent and the neighbouring towns of Vierville-sur-Mer and Asnières-en-Bessin, stirred by their desire to preserve the memory of these men, created an association named "Association du Souvenir des Commandos Britanniques" in 1991. Hence was born a new Franco-British memory, since the association also includes members from the Royal British Legion.

THE MEMORY OF WITNESSES

Unfortunately, there has never been any form of rigorous or systematic historical study based on the memory of those from Saint-Laurent-sur-Mer and Vierville-sur-Mer who took part in the events. This would have required that, shortly after the Liberation, witness accounts from those who saw or heard anything connected with operation Aquatint, as well as the reactions by the Germans and by the French authorities, be collected and recorded in writing. This was in fact done, alas too late, among the remaining accessible witnesses, but for many others, in particular those who had helped to hide the fugitives, a significant share of this private memory has been irremediably lost.[105]

This fragmentary and fragile memory did however circulate and, when the event finally aroused interest, after having been totally eclipsed for over forty years by the enormity of the D-Day landings on Omaha beach on the 6th of June 1944, it was finally revived and taken into consideration at the beginning of the 1980s. But, by then, so many of the witnesses had disappeared...

The result, today, is that many questions remain unanswered, several of which will very probably remain so forever. So what part of that local memory have we managed to preserve?

The Germans kept the civilian populations of Saint-Laurent and the neighbouring town of Vierville at a distance throughout the military enquiry, and they were totally forbidden any access to the funeral ceremony. Even if, during the night of the raid, all of the inhabitants of both towns and beyond, (Mme de

---

[105] **Several** important witnesses have **deceased** without any attempt to preserve, be it in writing or via any other audio or video medium, their account of the events: M Marcel Lemasson and M Paul de Brunville from Asnières-en-Bessin, Septime Humann from Juaye-Mondaye, Emmanuel Des Georges and Mme Suzanne Septavaux from Le Pin, who all offered assistance to Captain Graham Hayes. Furthermore, no attempts have been made to retrace the French people who helped Captain John Burton and Privates Jan Hellings and Adam Orr (Abraham Opoczynski), and consequently, to this day, we have no knowledge of where and in what circumstances these three **Aquatint** commandos were taken prisoner.

Falandre has confirmed this for Asnières-en-Bessin[106], and Mme Scelles, née Joss, for Sainte-Honorine-des-Pertes[107]) heard shelling and German machine gunfire, there were no, or very few, eye witnesses to the event.

Only a few Saint-Laurent inhabitants, the young Albert André, his father Félix André and his friend Edmond Scelles, at the time aged only 14, had managed to get a glimpse of the bodies on the beach at "Les Moulins". "One of them had been mutilated", recalled Albert André.[108]

As for André Legallois, he testified that two of the bodies had head wounds, apparently caused by gunshots.[109] He also saw the "three prisoners, exhausted, at the Kommandantur".

Another eye witness, M Paul Piprel, whose father owned the Hôtel du Casino in Vierville-sur-Mer, and who was only 16 in September 1942, was even requisitioned by a German to help him to transport one of the bodies to the top of the beach, to avoid the risk of the English soldier being washed away by the incoming tide. He was struck by a particular detail: the British soldier had no shoes and no waistbelt. He

---

[106] **Souvenirs de la guerre 1939-1945,** type-written text signed: **"Isabelle de Brunville**, wife of Martial Férault de Falandre", 3 pages 1996.

[107] Witness account that I personally collected on Tuesday 10th February 2004, at the home of M and Mme **Edmond Scelles**.

[108] Witness account collected by **Gilles Badufle** for his **video** in 1994.

[109] Idem

noticed no visible wounds. It could well have been the body of Major March-Phillips, who had very probably drowned.

Mme Frison, who lived close to "Les Moulins" from where the able-bodied prisoners had been driven by truck, heard one of them, almost certainly André Desgrange, shout out in French, "Don't worry, we'll be back!"[110]

Albert André also saw three prisoners in a German truck close to the beach. One of the soldiers said, again in French, "I'm not here for long', and he took from his pocket some French currency and ration stamps".[111]

On the 15th of September 1942, two inhabitants of Saint-Laurent, M Jules Scelles and a 1914-1918 veteran, both hidden behind a low wall next to the Hôtel du Carrefour, managed to get a glimpse of the funeral procession on its way to the cemetery and they heard the three gun salute that closed the ceremony. According to these witnesses, the coffins were placed on three carts, each of which was drawn by two horses, and all followed by a section of around thirty armed German soldiers. A wreath of flowers was placed on each coffin. Behind the convoy, there was a car from the Feldgendarmerie in Caen.[112]

---

[110] Extract from the article: "Opération **Aquatint**: un commando britannique débarque à Saint-Laurent-sur-Mer, du 12 au 13 septembre 1942", in **39-45 Magazine**, n° 65, September 1991, page 19.

[111] Witness account collected by Gilles Badufle for his video in 1994.

[112] 39-45 Magazine, page 19.

Albert André, who was then only 14, and who lived right next to the church and therefore to the cemetery, remembered having seen a German filming the convoy.[113] He also recalled that the coffins had been made from floorboards and shutters from an abandoned villa.

Another remarkable detail, this witness, together with M Edmond Scelles, both claimed to have seen the dog that had raised the alert, at the priory farm with a paw wound.

However, the witness account claiming that the same dog had been seen, held on leash by a German soldier, with an Iron Cross attached to its collar, would appear to be less reliable. Only Albert André claims to have seen the dog with such a medal.

Such are the rare direct witness accounts of the Saint-Laurent raid.

With the fortieth anniversary of the D-Day landings in 1984, the combined research of several people: André Heintz, English teacher in Caen, Marcel Leveel, retired from the S.N.C.F. (French railways) and founder of the Vierville-sur-Mer Museum and Mme de Falandre, offered the potential, for the first time since the Liberation, for the memory of the Aquatint raid to be officially acknowledged.

---

[113] *Witness account that I personally collected on Saturday 7th February 2004.*

▲
Mme Isabelle de Falandre (left) and **Mme Thérèse Chedal-Anglay**
(right) have gone to great lengths to obtain the official recognition of
the memory of **Aquatint**
They can be seen on this photograph, with **Wing Commander Brian
Spray**, after a ceremony held on the 21st of September 1985, before the
church and the cemetery in Saint-Laurent-sur-Mer. (Chedal-Anglay
Collection)

13801849

PTE. LEHNIGER, R.
PNR.CORPS

13.9.42

◄ *First grave of Richard Lehniger in Saint-Laurent-sur-Mer cemetery.*

Second grave of Richard Lehniger. Saint-Laurent-sur-Mer town cemetery, 2003. ▶

R. LEHNIGER SERVED AS
13801849 PRIVATE
R. LEONARD
PIONEER CORPS
COMMANDO
13TH SEPTEMBER 1942 AGE 42

LABOR OMNIA VINCIT

DIE INTERNATIONALE
WIRD DIE MENSCHHEIT SEIN

1985: the revival

One day, in 1985, M Mahieu, Mayor of Saint-Laurent-sur-Mer, fortuitously bumped into Richard Lehniger's daughter, Mrs Irene Walters who was accompanied by her husband and who was looking for her father's grave. Until then, no-one had managed to track down the raid's escapees or their families, with the exception of Graham Hayes' parents who had themselves contacted the de Brunville family in Asnières-en-Bessin as early as 1947.

A few weeks later, Mrs Walters sent biographical information on her father to Saint-Laurent's Mayor, for the latter was planning to commemorate, for the first time and in a grand fashion, the memory of the eleven men of whom three had fallen within his municipal territory.

Since the 1942 events, there had never been a single ceremony in Saint-Laurent specifically dedicated to them.

Encouraged by the Countess Isabelle de Falandre, M and Mme de Brunville's daughter and after great personal efforts and many contacts, M Mahieu succeeded in obtaining the participation of many personalities and dignitaries: the Sub-Prefect of Bayeux, M Legendre; Wing Commander Brian Spray (Royal Air Force), a representative from the British

Embassy in Paris, Lieutenant-Colonel Le Gall, who represented General Perrin, Commander of the 32nd Military Division; the Chairman of the D-Day Landing Committee, M Raymond Triboulet, Commanding Captain of the Bayeux Gendarmerie; the Superintendent of the American Cemetery in Colleville, Mr Joseph P. Rivers, representing General Donaldson, the standard bearers and members of veteran associations and of the Combattants Volontaires de la Résistance, and finally, the inhabitants of Saint-Laurent.

The ceremony began at 9.45 am on Saturday the 21st of September 1985 in Saint-Laurent Church with a Catholic service given by Dean Tourquetil and in the presence of the Protestant Minister, Edgar Fourez. The representative of the Israelite cult was unable to make the journey.

At 11 am, the personalities and the inhabitants of Saint-Laurent and its surrounding towns and villages were reunited in the small town cemetery next to the church. They had come to make and to listen to several speeches and to lay wreaths on the three British graves maintained by the Commonwealth Graves Commission.

As the town's Mayor, M Mahieu was the first to speak and he particularly emphasised the extraordinary life of Richard Lehniger *"an exceptional soldier who accomplished the supreme sacrifice in the name of freedom"*. Then Wing Commander Brian Spray expressed to the town's Mayor the *"immense gratitude of his country for the fidelity (...) and even the affection and brotherly love with which the inhabitants of Saint-Laurent-sur-Mer have kept alive, for 43 years now, the memory of the three members of the British Army who, during a hazardous operation which preceded by some twenty months the great D-Day landings of the 6th of June 1944, lost their lives on the municipal territory"*.

With great tact, the representative from the British Embassy in Paris briefly evoked the memory of Graham Hayes who was kept in hiding thanks to several members of the Resistance in Normandy.

He also revealed his burial place, in Viroflay town cemetery and, to close his speech, read the text engraved at the foot of his gravestone, *"Faithful even unto his death, he gave his life that we might live yet did not die!"*[114]

M Triboulet then intervened paying tribute to the memory of the three soldiers buried in the cemetery and he called to the young Norman population, unfortunately in small numbers at the ceremony, asking them to preserve the memory of each and every one of the combatants.

M Legendre, Sub-Prefect of Bayeux, concluded his speech with *"the courage, the heroism and the lessons to be learned from simple people, lost in combat, and*

---

[114] *Inscription engraved on Graham Hayes' grave in Viroflay town cemetery.*

although their deeds were isolated, we will never forget their immense sacrifice".[115]

After the laying of the wreaths, followed by the British and French national anthems played by the 32nd Infantry Regiment Military Band, the entire congregation was invited by the Mayor to a wine reception provided by the Saint-Laurent town council.

Places of memory and rites

From that day on, every year, the Mayor of Saint-Laurent and his town council have organised an official remembrance ceremony on the closest Sunday to the anniversary of the raid, in honour of the three British soldiers killed during the operation.

Up to 1992, the official ceremony, to which the local population is invited via press articles or personal invitation, revolved around three symbolic places: the church of Saint-Laurent where Mass is celebrated; the town cemetery where a short but always deeply moving commemoration takes place including the laying of wreaths, and the reception room where the wine reception is organised by the town council.

In the church, the standard bearers from various veteran associations are placed in the choir and Mass is read by Father Hamelin or Father Tourquetil, in presence of the Mayor, a few council representatives,

---

[115]*Quotation taken from the article published in **La Renaissance du Bessin**, n° 4240, Tuesday 24th September 1985, page 14.*

invited personalities and the local population. Of the three commandos buried in the cemetery, only Major March-Phillips was of Catholic profession, and he was in fact a particularly devoted Catholic. He often prayed. Two of his comrades in arms bore witness to his religious convictions after the war: Geoffrey Appleyard wrote, *"He's the first Army officer I've met so far who kneels down by the side of his bed for ten minutes before he goes to sleep"*.[116]

Before every commando operation, Tony Hall went to Anderson Manor chapel and he always found Gustavus March-Phillips there, *"I always felt frightened, and if one was involving oneself in something which was definitely possibly fatal being of my age, there was still time when one thought that the Church was the place one went to, and there was a chapel at Anderson, you see, and I remember I used to go and absolutely wet me knickers you see, but the thing was on the old old basis, you know, of don't let me be afraid and the last, the final night when we sort of took off and Gus didn't come back, I went there and hidden away in a corner was Gus as well. You know ..it helped me and if he saw me it must have helped him"*.[117]

Richard Lehniger and Alan Williams were, respectively, Jewish and Protestant. Since the isolated

---

[116] *Extract from the script broadcast by the **BBC** on the 20th of August 1971.*

[117] *Idem.*

ecumenical ceremony organised in 1985, each and every of the following ceremonies in Saint-Laurent church have been of Catholic profession.

During the ceremony, each of the three graves is adorned with the Union Jack. Behind the graves, facing the congregation, the standard bearers from the French and British patriotic associations are omnipresent: the local section of the Saint-Laurent-sur-Mer Veteran Society; the departmental section of the "Combattants Volontaires de la Résistance", the Normandy section of the "Jean-Marie Buckmaster" network, and finally, the Bramley section of the Royal British Legion.[118]

A speech is generally made by the Mayor, M Jean Martin from 1989 to 2001 and since then M Raymond Mouquet, recalling the circumstances around the operation. Then follows a short speech made by the Chairman of the Bramley section of the Royal British Legion.

A wreath donated by Saint-Laurent town council and artificial poppy wreaths brought by the Royal British Legion veterans are then laid at the foot of the graves, whilst observing one minute's silence. The silence is then broken by the Last Post played by the Trévières Fire Brigade Brass Band.

The third phase of the official remembrance ceremony is the gathering together of all participants to

---

[118] **Bramley is 4 miles to the north of Basingstoke, Hampshire.**

▲

M Raymond Mouquet, Mayor of Saint-Laurent-sur-Mer making a speech in the reception room of the Saint-Laurent-sur-Mer town hall, 15th September 2002. (Chedal-Anglay Collection)

share a glass of wine offered by Saint-Laurent town council, in the Town Hall reception room. Again, the Mayor makes a short speech, often to honour a distinguished invited guest. From 1989 to 2001, M Martin, who spoke excellent English, translated his speeches for the members of the Royal British Legion and for the British participants. His successor, M Mouquet, has his speeches translated by Mme Marie-Françoise Benoist, one of the town councillors.

The ceremonies have, on certain occasions, been particularly momentous in view of the personalities invited.

The great moments of Saint-Laurent's remembrance of Aquatint

In 1986, on the 13th of September, Lord Francis Howard of Penrith, his wife Anne and Henrietta March-Phillips all participated in the official ceremony to pay homage to the three commandos who had fallen on the beach of Saint-Laurent-sur-Mer. For this special occasion, M Mahieu, the town's Mayor, had invited M Roger Jouet, Vice-Chairman of the Conseil Général du Calvados, Mr Rivers, superintendent of the American Military Cemetery and Wing Commander Brian Spray who had already been present the previous year and who represented the British Embassy. It was the first time that an ex-member of the SSRF had come on an official visit to the precise location of the raid, 44 years after the event.

In 1992, a commemorative plaque, financed by the Royal British Legion veterans, was placed on the seafront, at the Commando's estimated landing spot, in order to solemnly commemorate the fiftieth anniversary of operation Aquatint. The inauguration ceremony took place on the 13th of September, in presence of M d'Harcourt, Member of Parliament for the Bayeux district, the superintendent of the American Military Cemetery in Colleville-sur-Mer, the Chief Brigadier of the Trévières Gendarmerie, a delegation of eight Royal British Legion veterans led by Mr Tony Evans, Chairman of the Bramley section, and seven members of Richard Lehniger's family including his widow and his daughter, Mrs Irene Walters.

The wooden framed plaque was engraved with the following bilingual inscription:

" En souvenir de l'opération **Aquatint** effectuée le 12 septembre 1942 par un commando britannique conduit par le Major March-Phillipps ".
(sic)
"This plaque is to commemorate the landing on 12th September 1942 of British Commandos led by Major March-Phillipps engaged on operation **Aquatint**. [119]

In 2001, the plaque was replaced by a bronze equivalent. Although the spot was of particular significance in the memory of Aquatint, since it was the closest to the actual spot where the commando landed

---

[119] *The text on this **plaque** includes **two errors**. In view of the landing time, the operation took place on the 13th and not the 12th of September. Furthermore, the surname of the operation's commander, March-Phillips, is misspelled with two "p". A few years later, the text was completely weatherbeaten and worn out and was replaced with a bronze plate. Unfortunately, the same mistakes were reproduced. The only modification was in fact the portion of the low wall on which the plaque is fixed which has been slightly raised.*

Inauguration of the first commemorative plaque on the seafront at Saint-Laurent-sur-Mer, 13th September 1992, presided by the Mayor, M Jean Martin. (Chedal-Anglay Collection)

in 1942, it had never been included in the official memorial ceremonies. Saint-Laurent's most recent Mayor, M Raymond Mouquet, decided to rectify that error during the 2003 ceremony on the 14th of September, by including the plaque as the first step in a genuine memorial tour which now leads the participants from the beach to the church, then to the cemetery and ending at the Town Hall.

As in 1986, the 1994 ceremony was to be one of the most exceptional events in the history of the Aquatint remembrance, since Tom Winter had made the trip to Saint-Laurent-sur-Mer. Tom, ex-member of the SSRF, was then the last survivor of the 1942 operation. At the age of 90, the ex Sergeant-Major had come back, for the very first time, to the spot where he had been taken prisoner some fifty-two years earlier. After the official ceremony in the cemetery, more poignant than in previous years in reason of his presence, followed by a brief religious service in the church, Tom Winter was invited by the Mayor, together with his compatriot Leslie Wright, to a more intimate ceremony in the Town Hall reception room. The Mayor then awarded them with the fiftieth anniversary commemorative medal donated by the Lower Normandy Regional Council (Conseil Régional de Basse-Normandie) and given to all allied veterans.

Two high school teachers from Trévières[120] took advantage of Tom Winter's presence by interviewing him and asking him questions on operation Aquatint in front of a camera. Together with their 3rd form pupils, they were working on a school project which involved

---

[120] In 1994, when **Tom Winter** travelled to Saint-Laurent-sur-Mer, two secondary school teachers from Trévières High School, Gilles Badufle, History-Geography teacher and Pierre Poutaraud, PE teacher, made an hour-long film on the **Aquatint** raid within the context of a **Projet d'Action Educative** (P.A.E.), Educative Action Project. For the occasion, witness reports (André Legallois, Pierre Piprel, Edmond Scelles), and the account of the only surviving commando member, Tom Winter, were collected, 52 years after the event. The film is of good quality despite the amateur equipment used, and is an important constituent of the **collective memory of operation Aquatint in Normandy.**

putting together a video on the 1942 raid. The film was publicly projected the following year on Saturday the 9th of September at the VVF (holiday camp) in Colleville-sur-Mer, in the presence of the Mayor, M Martin and the author Gilles Perrault, renowned for many successful publications including Le Secret du Jour J.[121]

The year 1997 was marked by the presence of Austen Hayes, Captain Graham Hayes' youngest brother, together with an important delegation from the Royal British Legion. On certain photographs, the resemblance between the two men is striking.

During the ceremony on the 14th of September, following the minute's silence and the Last Post, Austen Hayes had requested to read a speech in memory of his brother Graham, shot down by the Nazis on the 13th of July 1943. It was a moment of shared and intense emotion, during which the last member of the Hayes family and of the event's contemporaries, wished to thank, once more and publicly this time, the de Brunville family, represented by Mme de Falandre, who had hidden his brother whilst he awaited his transfer with the help of other members of the Normandy Resistance.

However, the memory of Aquatint would perhaps never have survived so durably if the decision had not been made, fifteen years ago, to create a remembrance association.

[121] Gilles Perrault, **Le secret du jour J**, Librairie Arthème Fayard, Paris, 1964.

Austen Hayes, Graham's brother, making a speech in Saint-Laurent cemetery, 12th September 1997. (Chedal-Anglay Collection)

ASSOCIATIVE REMEMBRANCE

Strong and close links had been woven over several years between the French families and the British families, members of the Royal British Legion, and it appeared essential that a living memory be maintained of an event that had so often been pushed into the background behind the commemorations of the D-Day landings on the 6th of June 1944. A new interest was emerging among Normans for this previously unknown WWII event. It was therefore vital that all of the energy and good will available be reunited to preserve this memory for as long as possible.

M Jean Martin, Mayor of Saint-Laurent, who succeeded the founder of the 1985 ceremony, M Mahieu, assumed and totally fulfilled this remembrance obligation. During a general meeting, together with M Marcel Levéel from Vierville-sur-Mer, he formed an association ruled by the French 1901 law on associations and called, "Association du Souvenir des Commandos Britanniques, A.S.C.B. (Normandie 1940-1944)", "Association in Memory of the British Commandos (Normandy 1940-1944)", and whose articles were submitted to the Sub-Prefecture in Bayeux on the 22nd of October 1991.

Article 2 gives the association's main aim, *"(…) to maintain the memory of the operations carried out on the Normandy coast by British commandos during the period 1940-1944, and in particular of operation Aquatint by the Small Scale Raiding Force"*. The association's head office is situated within the Saint-Laurent Town Hall. The association's creation was published in the 11th December 1991 issue of the **French Official Journal**.

The British veterans and the members of the Bramley section of the Royal British Legion, who expressed such a desire, are mentioned in article 4 as being "honorary members" of the association. At the members' Annual General Meeting, M Martin and M Levéel were respectively elected Chairman and Secretary of the ASCB.

The association is led by dynamic and enthusiastic members, among whom M Jean-Pierre Chedal-Anglay and his wife Thérèse, and concentrates its activities around the welcoming of the Bramley section of the Royal British Legion and their families, on the closest weekend to the raid's anniversary date. The British families are dispatched among Normandy families willing and able to accommodate them; a programme of excursions is organised on the Saturday and a gala lunch is held on the Sunday after the official ceremony.

On some years, as was the case in 1985, the English families in Bramley welcome the French families, thus forming a sort of twinning between this small Hampshire town and the towns of Saint-Laurent-sur-Mer-Vierville-sur-Mer, based on the memory of the Aquatint commandos.

In March 2003, M Alain Godet was elected Chairman of the ASCB, replacing M Jean Martin who did not wish to renew his mandate. This transfer was the opportunity to add two new ingredients to the official remembrance day, jointly organised with the new Mayor of Saint-Laurent-sur-Mer, M Raymond Mouquet: the laying of a wreath at the commemorative plaque on the seafront and the playing of the Last Post by an adolescent from Trévières.

After twelve years official existence, the ASCB now includes 35 members half of whom experienced the war or were born shortly after 1945. Just like many other memorial associations with similar aims, the question of its longevity remains. The 2004 ceremony, held on Sunday 12th September reunited at least one

M Alain Godet, Chairman of the Association du Souvenir des Commandos Britanniques, making a speech before the British graves of Saint-Laurent-sur-Mer, 14th September 2003.
(Chedal-Anglay Collection)

hundred participants. The challenge for the new chairman and the association's active members will be to maintain and develop its attractiveness in order to keep the memory of the Aquatint commandos alive for as long as possible in the collective memory among the Normandy population. Let us hope that the publication of this book will provide a further contribution to the accomplishment of their aim.

All of the members of the Small Scale Raiding Force were tough charactered, strong personalities, with varying geographical, social and religious origins, but each and every one of them engaging, all reunited by the same steadfast friendship, the same taste for danger and adventure, the same faith in victory.

Eleven of them set out to land during that night of the Occupation, on the 12th of September 1943, on the Saint-Laurent-sur-Mer beach. Four of them lost their lives on French soil, and three of them now lay to rest in Normandy where they have never been forgotten.

One of the men, Gustavus March-Phillips, who was not only the group's commander but also a highly admired and respected man, left us with a poem, written at the time of the Maid Honor Force's African epic.

Be it pure coincidence or premonition, the poem begins with the words *"If I must die"* and constitutes a genuine spiritual testament. It bears witness to the deep faith and the incandescent hope of a man who held high the colours of honour and courage.

"If I must die…"

If I must die in this great war,
When so much seems in vain,
And man in huge unthinking hordes
Is slain as sheep are slain,
But with less thought; then do I seek
One last good grace to gain.

Let me die, Oh Lord, as I learned to live
When the world seemed young and gay,
And "Honour Bright" was a phrase they used
That they do not use today,
And faith was something alive and warm
When we gathered round to pray.

Grave of Richard Lehniger
Saint-Laurent-sur-Mer town
cemetery, 2003.

Grave of Major G. H. March-
Phillips, D.S.O., M.B.E.,
Saint-Laurent-sur-Mer town
cemetery, 2003.

Let me be simple and sure once more,
Oh Lord if I must die,
Let the mad unreason of reasoned doubt,
Unreasoning, pass me by,
And the mass mind, and the mercenary,
And the everlasting 'why'.

Let me be brave and gay again,
Oh Lord, when my time is near,
Let the good in me rise up and break
The stranglehold of fear;
Say that I die for Thee and the King,
And what I hold most dear.

G. March-Phillips, 1941

Grave of Alan Williams. Saint-Laurent-sur-Mer town cemetery, 2003.

Sources

I PUBLIC ARCHIVES

A/ PUBLIC ARCHIVES OUTSIDE OF FRANCE

British National Archives (Public Record Office, Kew)

Special Operations Executive Records (HS):

- HS 3/77: S.O.E. West Africa, Final Report Fernando Po and Spanish Guinea.
- HS 3/86: S.O.E. West Africa, 1941, Operation Postmaster, Removal of Italian Merchant Ship and Two Germans Vessels from Harbour of Santa Isabel, Fernando Po.
- HS 3/87: S.O.E. West Africa, Postmaster, ditto.
- HS 3/88: 1942-1947, Postmaster, Summary of Maid Honor Operations.
- HS 3/89: 1941-1942, Postmaster, Report on Operation.
- HS 3/93: Operation Postmaster, Recommandations for, and Correspondence arising from Awards, Decorations and Promotions.

Admiralty, Naval Forces, Royal Marines, Coastguard and Related Bodies (ADM) Records:

- ADM 179/227: Operation Aquatint: Report on Raid on Sainte-Honorine carried out by Small Scale Raiding Party, 1942.

Ministry of Defence (DEFE) Records:

- DEFE 2: Combined Operations Headquarters, and Ministry of Defence, Combined Operations Headquarters later Amphibious Warfare Headquarters: Records 1937-1963.
- DEFE 2/109: "Brandford", "Dryad", "Musketoon", "Fahrenheit", "Barricade", "Aquatint", "Facsimile", "Basalt" and "Batman", Vol. 1A.
- DEFE 2/365: "Musketoon", "Barricade" and "Aquatint", 1942.

GERMAN MILITARY ARCHIVES, FRIBOURG (BUNDESARCHIV-MILITÄRARCHIV FREIBURG)

716 Infanterie-Division

- RH 26-716/4 (24-183/1): Tätigkeitsbericht des Ia zum KTB Nr. 1 vom 1.5.41-31.10.42 (Activity report of).
- RH 26-716/2 (24-183/2a): Englishes Landungsunternehmen bei Stützpunkt 29 St. Laurent am 13.9.42 (English raid on Strong point 29 in Saint-Laurent on 13.9.42).
- RH 26-716/ (39-431/9): Tätigkeitsberichte des Ic (Feindtätigkeit) zum KTB 1 vom 1.9.42-30.9.43 (Activity reports from the Ic) (Enemy activity).

German press
- *Volkischer Beobachter*, 21st January 1942 (article and photo on the Fernando Po affair).

British press
- *Yorks Evening Post*, 18th February 1943 (article on the D.S.O. attributed to Major Appleyard), 7th September 1943 (article on the disappearance of Major Appleyard), 8th November 1948 (article on the Memorial consecrated on the 7th of November 1948 in Linton church).
- *The Daily Telegraph*, 8th December 1999 (Lord Howard of Penrith necrology article).
- *Times Group Newspapers*, 22nd March 1984 (article on Leslie Wright's participation in the Maid Honor Force).

B/ FRENCH PUBLIC ARCHIVES

FRENCH NATIONAL ARCHIVES, PARIS

1374 W 39: Audition of Robert Kieffer, 27th August 1944 and of Roger Bardet, 20th September 1944.
72 AJ 41: Bill of indictment against Roger Bardet, 5th December 1949.

Press collections

- 13 T I /170 / 6: *La Presse Caennaise*, 16th September 1942 (Dispatch on the Aquatint raid).

- 13 T I /171 /7: *Le Journal de Normandie*, 15th September 1942 (Idem).

- 13 T I/174 /9: *Liberté de Normandie*, 7-8-9-11/12-13-15-18/19 December 1949 (Bardet-Kieffer court case).

- 13 T I /176 /11: *Ouest France*, 6-7-8-9-10/11-12-13-14-16/17 December 1949 (Idem).

- 13 T II/29/31: *Journal de Bayeux*, 18th September 1942 (Dispatch on the Aquatint raid).

- 13 T II/31/7: *Le Courrier du Bessin*, 17th to 24th September 1942, (Idem).

- 13 T VII/401: *Ouest-Eclair*, 15th September 1942 (Ibid.).

Reports by the Sub-Prefect of Bayeux and the Prefect of Calvados

- 726 W 16817: Reports by the Sub-Prefect of Bayeux, September 1941 to December 1942.

- 726 W 16857: Sub-Prefecture of Bayeux: German occupation.

- Information report by the Prefect of Calvados, Michel Cacaud, dated 4th November 1942, addressed to the Head of State, Minister, Secretary of State for the

Interior and to the Regional Prefect in Rouen, in ***Rapports du préfet du Calvados de 1939 à 1944***, Direction des Archives du Calvados.

Archives from the Departmental Service of the Office National des Anciens Combattants et Victimes de Guerre du Calvados (National Veteran and War Victim Office, Calvados).

- Fonds Mirey.

- Attestation by Mme Suzanne Septavaux sent to the O.N.A.C. in Calvados, on the 11th of June 1959, in support of the CVR request (Voluntary Resistance Fighter medal) concerning Mr Septime Humann.

II PRIVATE ARCHIVES

BBC ARCHIVES

- Script for a radio programme broadcast by the BBC on the 20th August 1971, from 10.30 am to 11.30 am, entitled: "If any question why we died (A quest for March-Phillips)" The script was based on recordings made by Henrietta March-Phillips and comprises 29 type-written pages.

London Gazette Archives

- Supplement to the London Gazette, 28th January 1943, page 526.

André Heintz' personal Archives including:
Correspondence from:

- Charles Howe (First owner of the Maid Honor) to Leslie Wright, dated 26th January 1984,

- Charles Messenger to André Heintz, dated 18th February 1985,

- Isabelle De Falandre to André Heintz, dated 15th January 1985, 27th March 1986, 20th April 1986, 10th December 1986, 7th February 1997, 7th March 1997, 13th January 1999 and 11th October 1999,

- Henrietta March-Phillips to André Heintz, dated 4th June 1985,

- Lord Francis Howard of Penrith to André Heintz, dated 3rd December 1985,

- Tom Winter to André Heintz, dated 23rd January 1986,

- Tony Hall to André Heintz, dated 30th January 1986,

- Leslie Wright to Charles Howe, dated 11th February 1986,

- Ian Dear to André Heintz, dated 28th February 1986,

- Anne Burton to André Heintz, dated 11th September 1986,

- Anne Burton to Isabelle de Falandre, dated 21st October 1986,

- Mike Langley to Brian Spray, dated 24th November 1986,

- Brian Spray to André Heintz, dated 27th November 1986,

- Austen Hayes to Isabelle de Falandre, dated 21st December 1996, 9th January 1997,
- Duncan Stuart to Isabelle de Falandre, dated 14th January 1997, 20th February 1997,
- Duncan Stuart to André Heintz, dated 24th November 1999,
- Erich Dehn to André Heintz, dated 15th July 2003,
- Anne Howard of Penrith to André Heintz, dated 20th July 2003,
- Irene Walters to André Heintz, dated 21st July and 24th September 2003,
- Jane Hall to André Heintz, dated 31st July 2003
- Denis Mason Jones to André Heintz, dated 9th January 2004,
- Mike Langley to André Heintz, dated 20th August, 15th September 1986, 15th August 1988 and May 2004.

BIBLIOGRAPHY

I On the Special Operations Executive (SOE)

- Foot M.R.D., **S.O.E. in France, An account of the work of the British Special Operations Executive in France 1940-1944**, London, Her Majesty's Stationery Office, 1966, 550 pages, republished by White Hall History Publishing, 2004.

- Cookridge E.H., **"Mettez le feu à l'Europe" (Churchill)**, Fayard, Paris, 1968.

- Foot M.R.D., SOE: **The Special Operations Executive 1940-46**, B.B.C., London, 1984.

- Ruby Marcel, **La guerre secrète, Les réseaux Buckmaster**, Editions France-Empire, Paris, 1985, 275 pages.

- Wilkinson Peter and Astley Bright, **Gubbins and S.O.E.**, Leo Cooper, London, 1993.

- Brooks Richard, **Secret Flotillas, The Clandestine Sea Lines to France and French North Africa 1940-1944**, London, HMSO, 1996, 729 pages, translated into French by Pierrick Roullet, under the title **Flottilles secrètes, Les liaisons maritimes clandestines en France et en Afrique du nord, 1940-1944**, Editions M.D.V., Le Touvet, 2001, 959 pages.

II On the British commandos (including the Small Scale Raiding Force)

- Appleyard J.E., **Geoffrey: Major John Geoffrey Appleyard, DSO, MC and Bar, MA of the Commandos and Special Air Service Regiment**, Whitehead & Miller, Leeds, 1945, Blandford Press, 1946.
- Saunders St-George Hilary, **The Green Beret**, White Lion Publisher Ltd, 1949, 1972.
- Cruickshank Charles, **The German Occupation of The Channel Islands**, The Guernsey Press Co. Ltd, 1975.
- Messenger Charles, **The Commandos, 1940-1946**, William Kimber, London, 1985, 447 pages.
- Langley Mike, **Anders Lassen, V.C., M.C., of the S.A.S.**, New English Library, London, 1988, 254 pages.
- Martin Jean, **Les commandos britanniques de la Seconde Guerre mondiale**, available from the author, undated, 112 pages.
- Dear Ian, **Sabotage & Diversion and OSS at War**, Cassell, London, 1996.
- Guillou Michel, **L'opération "Fahrenheit"**, http://perso.wanadoo.fr/passion.histoire/fahren.htm, 13 pages.
- Fry Helen, **Jews in North Devon during the Second World War**, Halsgrove, 2005, 160 pages

III On the Resistance in France and in Normandy

- Noguères Henri, in collaboration with Marcel Degliame-Fouché and Jean-Louis Vigier, **Histoire de la Résistance en France**, including:

- Tome 1: juin 1940-juin 1941, Robert Laffont, Paris, 1967, 510 pages.

- Tome 2: juillet 1941-octobre 1942, Robert Laffont, Paris, 1969, 733 pages.

- Lilienfeld Jean-Marie, **La Résistance et la répression allemande dans le Calvados, 1940-1944**, Diplôme d'Etudes Supérieures d'Histoire, juin 1966, 95 pages + appendices.

- Baudot Marcel, **Libération de la Normandie**, Hachette Littérature, Paris, 1974, 255 pages.

- Leclerc Marcel, **La Résistance dans la Manche**, réseaux et mouvements, Edition de la Dépêche, Cherbourg, 1982, 290 pages, republished by Editions Eurocibles, Marigny, 2004.

- Mazeline André, **Clandestinité, La Résistance dans le département de l'Orne**, Editions Tirésias, Paris, 1994, 203 pages (re-edition of the first book published by an editor in La Ferté-Macé in 1947)

- Quellien Jean, Vico Jacques, **Massacres nazis en Normandie, Les fusillés de la prison de Caen**, Condé-sur-Noireau, Charles Corlet éditions, 1994, 234 pages, republished 2004.

IV On the Interallié and Jean-Marie/Donkeyman networks

- Borchers Erich (Major), **Abwehr contre Résistance**, Amiot-Dumont, Paris, 1949, 206 pages.

- Young Gordon, **L'espionne n° 1: La Chatte**, Arthème Fayard, Paris, 1957, republished by Editions J'ai Lu, Flammarion, Paris, 1968, 185 pages.

- Carré Mathilde-Lily, **J'ai été "La Chatte"**, Editions Morgan, Paris, 1959, 290 pages.

- Reile Oscar, **Geheime Westfront**, Verlag Welsermühl, München und Wels, 1962, translated into French by R. Jouan, under the title: **L'Abwehr, Le contre-espionnage allemand en France**, Editions France-Empire, Paris, 1970, 316 pages.

- Bleicher Hugo, (German title unknown), Adolf Sponholz, Hanover, 217 pages, translated into French under the title: **Le récit du sergent Bleicher, monsieur Jean**, 124 pages, and in English under the title: **Colonel Henri's Story: The War Memoirs of Hugo Bleicher**, Editions William Kimber, 1954, republished Ian Colvin 1968.

- Bouffay Gaëtane et alii, **Visages lexoviens, 1940-1945**, duplicated, undated (vers 1975), 123 pages.

V On operation Aquatint

- "Opération Aquatint. Un commando britannique débarque à Saint-Laurent-sur-Mer du 12 au 13 septembre 1942", **39-45 magazine**, n° 65, 4th quarter 1991, pages 13-21.

ACKNOWLEDGEMENTS

To the following...

- Albert André, retired, ex-secretary of the "L'Association du Souvenir des Commandos Britanniques (Normandy 1940-1944)", (A.S.C.B.),
- Annie Balmas-Rousselot, Conservator of the Montbéliard Media and Reference Library
- Laurent Bastard, Director of the Musée du Compagnonnage in Tours,
- Philippe Bauduin, historian, ex-Director of the A.N.V.A.R. (National Agency for the Valorisation of Research)
- Sephton Baxter, Chairman of the Linton-on-Wharfe "Village Hall" Committee,
- Henri Beaudet, retired farmer, ex-Chairman of the Amicale du Réseau "Jean-Marie" Buckmaster de Normandie (Normandy Jean-Marie/Buckmaster Network Association)
- Marie-Claude Berthelot, Musée Mémorial de Caen, scientific centre, librarian in charge of printed and manuscript documents, Caen,
- Jean-Pierre Chedal-Anglay, E.C.P. Engineer, and Thérèse Chedal-Anglay, housewife, Vierville-sur-Mer,
- Jacques Comby, ex-Naval Officer,
- Eric Dehn, honorary professor of Bristol Grammar School,
- Christian Dereims, honorary professor and Regional Pedagogical Inspector for German studies,
- David J. Drew, honorary professor of Rickmansworth Grammar School,
- Eugène Dufouil, Chairman of the Association des Marins et Anciens Marins Combattants d'Angers et Région, Angers (Angers Sailors and Veteran Sailors Association)
- The Count and Countess Martial Férault de Falandre,
- Françoise Fournier, trilingual secretary, Le Mans,
- Alain Godet, retired solicitor, Chairman of the "Association du Souvenir des Commandos Britanniques (Normandie 1940-1944)", (A.S.C.B.),
- Denis Grisel, Director of the Doubs Departmental Archives,
- Tony Hall, ex-SSRF commando, and his wife Jane,
- Patrick Hautechaud, telecommunications manager, Chairman of the Amicale du Réseau Jean-Marie Buckmaster de Normandie (Normandy Jean-Marie/Buckmaster Network Association),

- Austen Hayes, Graham Hayes' youngest brother, artist,
- The Lord Francis Howard of Penrith, ex-SSRF commando, and Lady Anne Howard of Penrith, his wife,
- David Howson, Treasurer of the Linton-on-Wharfe, "Village Hall" Committee,
- Christian Hurel, professor emeritus from the Faculty of Ondotology, University of Marseille,
- Eliane Marchand, Conservator at the Montbéliard Town Archives,
- Denis Mason Jones,
- Mike Langley, writer,
- Louis Le Roc'h Morgère, Director of the Calvados Departemental Archives,
- Henrietta March-Phillips, daughter of Commander Gustavus March-Phillips,
- Jean Martin, ex-Mayor of Saint-Laurent-sur-Mer, founding member of the Association du Souvenir des Commandos Britanniques (Normandie 1940-1944), (A.S.C.B.),
- Raymond Mouquet, retired engineer, Mayor of Saint-Laurent-sur-Mer, and his wife,
- Adrien Pattinson, ex-Chairman of the Launton-Gavray twinning committee
- Philippe Pique, Editor, O.R.E.P. Edition & Communication, Cully,
- The Viscount and Viscountess Joël du Pontavice,
- Edmond Scelles, retired farmer, and his wife,
- Sebastian Scherr,
- Brian Spray, ex-Wing Commander, Royal Air Force,
- Duncan Stuart, ex-SOE receiver (SOE Adviser),
- Jacques Vico, Vice-President of the Confédération Nationale des Combattants Volontaires de la Résistance, President of the Calvados Section
- Irene and John Walters, daughter and son-in-law of Richard Lehniger,
- Tom Winter, ex-SSRF commando,
- Leslie Wright, ex-commando.

…. we would like to express our most genuine and sincere gratitude…

… as well as to our wives who have shown great patience and understanding.

INDEX

Summary

Born in 1956 in Le Mans, **Gérard Fournier** obtained a doctorate in history from the Pantheon Sorbonne University in Paris in 1989, and has taught history and geography for over twenty years in secondary schools in Caen, Normandy. He taught in Potigny High School (Calvados) from 1984 to 2000, and, since then, has taught in Hastings High School in Caen where he founded and now runs a study group entitled "Memoirs and History of the two world wars", in partnership with Buvignier High School in Verdun (Meuse region).

Project leader for the Calvados Departmental Archives (educational department) from 1990 to 1996, then again in 2003, he was detached by the Ministry of Education, from 1996 to 2000, to study the Archives du Monde Combattant (World Veteran Archives) held by the Defence Ministry, on behalf of the FMD, the Fondation pour la Mémoire de la Déportation (Deportation Memorial Foundation), and to lead a group of researchers in charge of the drafting of Le Livre-Mémorial des déportés de France arrêtés par mesures de répression 1940-1945, published by the FMD in 2004 **(Memorial Book of the French deported and arrested as a method of repression from 1940 to 1945)**.

Gérard Fournier is the author of several publications covering, initially, the history of the working-classes. Besides his thesis entitled: "Master tanners and labourers in Château-Renault, from the middle of the 18th Century to 1914" (unpublished), he has also published, in particular, within **the Cahiers des Archives Départementales du Calvados**, n° 7, 1996, "Une famille de tanneurs: les Pellerin de Bonnebosq" (A family of tanners, the Pellerin de Bonnebosq) and in **the Annales de Normandie**, March 2002, "Une industrie autrefois florissante: la tannerie de Bayeux" (A formerly flourishing industry: the Bayeux tannery). He is also the co-author of **Potigny, Terre d'immigration**, Le Livre de l'Année, 1999, and **Les mondes souterrains, Histoire de l'exploitation du sous-sol du Calvados**, Direction des Archives du Calvados, 2003.

His other great prediliction is the history of the Second World War. He has published, in particular Le Calvados sous l'Occupation **(Calvados under occupation)**, Direction des Archives du Calvados, 1993 and **Si près de la Liberté (So close to freedom) in memory of Father Bousso and his Resistance companions executed on June 6th 1944 in Caen, Association Hommage à l'Abbé Bousso, 1994.** He is also the author of two papers, on the "Déportés du Calvados" (the Calvados deported), published in the proceedings of the 1995 **international conference "De la fin des camps à la reconstruction, Les Normands 1945-1947"** (From the end of the camps to reconstruction, the Normans 1945-1947) published in 2001 by the Calvados Archives, and the other on "Le rôle de la Résistance normande dans la réussite du Débarquement", (The role of the Normandy Resistance in the success of the D-Day landings), published in the proceedings of the 2004 **international conference on "Les populations civiles dans le Jour J et la bataille de Normandie"**, (Civilian population on D-Day and during the battle of Normandy) Caen Mémorial, 2005.

And finally, Gérard Fournier has contributed to the production of two CD-Roms on La **Résistance dans la Calvados** (the Resistance in Calvados), AERI, 2004 and La **Résistance dans l'Orne** (the Resistance in Orne), AERI, 2005, as well as a DVD-Rom on **the 60ème anniversaire du Débarquement et de la bataille de Normandie** (60th Anniversary of the D-Day landings and the Battle of Normandy) SCEREN-CRDP of Basse-Normandie, 2004.

André Heintz was born in Caen in 1920 where he pursued his secondary and further education. As a member of the Resistance (Civil and Military Organisation and Northern Liberation) during the German occupation, he played an active role, with the emergency services, in evacuating the wounded towards the Bon Sauveur hospital during the battle of Caen. After the liberation, he immediately joined a British civil affairs detachment for which he served as interpreter for five months.

After spending two years as an Assistant at the University of Edinburgh, André Heintz returned to Caen to teach English at the Lycée Malherbe (1947 - 1965), including a two year stay in the United States. Member of the Comité d'Histoire de la Seconde Guerre mondiale (the Second World War History Committee), he continued his research after his retirement. He remains the correspondent of many British historians.

Author of several books and articles on the battle of Normandy, André Heintz has published, among others: with Marcel Leclerc, **La Manche 1940-1944**, Editions Libro-Sciences, 1978; with Jean Collin, **La vie quotidienne des étudiants à l'Université de Caen de 1939 à 1955**, (The daily life of Caen University students from 1939 to 1955) Caen University Press, 1994. He also contributed to several joint publications: "Caen pendant la bataille: récit d'un témoin", (Caen during the battle: a witness account) in **Normandie 44**, Institut d'Histoire du Temps Présent, Albin Michel, 1987; "Un membre de la Croix Rouge et de la Résistance raconte...", (A member of the Red Cross and the Resistance recounts...) in **Témoignages, Récits de la vie caennaise, 6 juin-19 juillet 1944**, Ville de Caen, 1984; "L'eau et les civils pendant la bataille de Caen", (Water and civilians during the battle of Caen) in **L'eau à la source de la victoire 1944**, Editions Saecno, 1994.

- Commandeur des Palmes Académiques,
- Chevalier de l'Ordre du Mérite,
- Médaille du Combattant Volontaire de la Résistance.

This publication was supported by the
Conseil régional de Basse-Normandie
and the Centre régional des Lettres de Basse-Normandie.

15 rue de Largerie - 14480 Cully, France
Tel: 02 31 08 31 08
Fax: 02 31 08 31 09
E-mail: info@orep-pub.com
Web: www.orep-pub.com

Graphic conception: OREP
ISBN: 2-915762-05-8
Copyright OREP 2006
All rights reserved

Legal deposit 2nd term 2006

Printed in France